The TIME Is NOW! Series

BATTLE CRY FOR YOUR MARRIAGE

Discovering Breakthroughs for Today's Challenges

Larry and LaVerne Kreider
Steve and Mary Prokopchak
Duane and Reyna Britton
Wallace and Linda Mitchell

House To House Publications
Lititz, Pennsylvania USA
www.h2hp.com

Books in This Series
When God Seems Silent
Battle Cry for Your Marriage
Straight Talk To Leaders

Books in this series coming soon
Finding Freedom and Staying Free!
Experiencing the Supernatural

Battle Cry for Your Marriage
Discovering Breakthroughs for Today's Challenges

by Larry and LaVerne Kreider, Steve and Mary Prokopchak,
Duane and Reyna Britton, Wallace and Linda Mitchell

Copyright © 2016 Larry and LaVerne Kreider, Steve and Mary
Prokopchak, Duane and Reyna Britton, Wallace and Linda Mitchell

Published by
House to House Publications
11 Toll Gate Road, Lititz, PA 17543 USA
Telephone: 800.848.5892
www.h2hp.com

ISBN 10: 0-9904293-8-5
ISBN-13: 978-0-9904293-8-8

Unless otherwise noted, all scripture quotations in this publication are
taken from the *Holy Bible, New International Version* (NIV).
© 1973, 1978, 1984 by International Bible Society. Used by permission
of Zondervan Publishing House. All rights reserved.

CONTENTS

How to Use This Resource

Personal study

Read from start to finish and receive personal revelation. Learn spiritual truths to help yourself and others.

- Each reading includes questions for personal reflection and room to journal at the end of the book.
- Each chapter has a key verse to memorize.

Daily devotional

Eight weeks of daily readings with corresponding questions for personal reflection and journaling.

- Each chapter is divided into seven sections for weekly use.
- Each day includes reflection questions and space to journal.

Mentoring relationship

Questions can be answered and life applications discussed when this book is used as a one-on-one discipling/mentoring tool.

- A spiritual mentor can easily take a person they are mentoring through these short Bible study lessons and use the reflection questions for dialogue about what is learned.
- Study each day's entry or an entire chapter at a time.

Small group study

Study in a small group setting or in a class or Bible study group.

- The teacher teaches the material using the outline provided at the end of the book. Everyone in the group reads the chapter and discusses the questions together.

Introduction

There is a battle cry for healthy marriages in our generation! Before military leaders move their troops, a battle plan is required. We believe a battle plan is also necessary to protect and promote healthy marriages in our generation. Marriage relationships need practical and proven biblical strategies to meet today's challenges. Our prayer is that this book will help you and your spouse discover fresh insights, wisdom and change that lead you to God's best for your relationship.

The couples who have joined us (Larry and LaVerne) to write this book have not only experienced God's blessing in their marriages but have also gone through their own journey of learning to love through difficult times. Each author models and ministers the lessons and marriage principles you will read about in this book. Many of us have years of experience offering personal marriage counseling as well as speaking at marriage seminars throughout the USA and in multiple other nations.

May you find the biblical principles, stories and life lessons in this book valuable and encouraging as you take steps to keep a healthy marriage relationship.

Remember, there is no perfect marriage, but we serve the creator of marriage and He is perfect. Each of the authors is praying that you will benefit from their mistakes and what they have learned. Finally, each of us desires you to experience a prosperous marriage that draws you closer to one another and to God.

God's absolute best to you!

— *Larry and LaVerne Kreider, Steve and Mary Prokopchak, Duane and Reyna Britton, Wallace and Linda Mitchell*

CHAPTER 1

Trying to Fix Your Spouse "Ain't Gonna Work"

Larry and LaVerne Kreider

Never Stop Dating

When Larry and I met, I was 14 years of age and in the ninth grade. My parents asked me to wait until I was 16 and a half to begin dating, but Larry and I found ways to be together that were not necessarily a real date. For example, whenever we could, we went ice skating at the popular skating spot on the lake near my house. Our status as high school sweethearts became a bit more serious when we actually started dating "officially."

On our first real date, Larry took me shopping and to a restaurant. What fun! But after we married, our relaxing times together became almost nonexistent. Instead our days were filled with work and our evenings with youth ministry to unchurched teens. Today we both realize that our most important relationship outside of our relationship with God should be our marriage. Unfortunately at the time, no one mentored us in this all-important direction. Our focus was on good and necessary things—work and outreach ministry—but not on our marriage. Consequently our relationship waned.

I (Larry) thought LaVerne was the problem. When we finally went for marriage counseling, we found we had to make some serious changes in our lives.

Our marriage counselor quickly picked up on one of our main problems. I was not making any attempts at meeting the emotional needs of the woman God gave to me. I soon realized that I needed to take whatever time was needed to communicate with LaVerne in a way that she felt cherished and loved. She needed to know that she was a priority in my life.

I (LaVerne) also realized that my identity and worth needed to be in Christ first, and that it was not possible for Larry to fulfill all of my needs. I soon began to realize that I could only find complete fulfillment in Jesus Christ and in my Heavenly Father's love for me. Although it really helped when Larry began to communicate with me in a way that I felt cherished, I could not demand this from him.

The scriptures tell us: "Do not be deceived, God is not mocked; for whatever a man sows, that he will also reap" (Galatians 6:7). We found this truth also applies to our marriage relationship. We made a conscious decision to sow into our marriage like we did when we were dating. We took a weekend away together with a ministry called Marriage Encounter, where I learned to put into writing my feelings for LaVerne. I also learned to describe word pictures, sharing my feelings, not just facts. It really stretched me because I am not normally a "feeling" kind of a guy. I am more of a "fact" guy. Sharing feelings made me feel vulnerable. But this exercise was life changing for

> Our focus was on good and necessary things— work and outreach ministry— but not on our marriage.

both of us: we began to better understand one another and our emotional needs.

Proverbs 5:18 says, "Rejoice with the wife of your youth." This verse does not mean only when a wife is young but continually throughout life.

LaVerne and I started dating again. We planned for a date night at least once a month. We found another couple who also desired to date monthly, so we swapped babysitting services for free, which worked great! Now we are in our mid-sixties, still dating.

REFLECTION
Why do we need to date?

We also decided to get away together overnight every anniversary to keep our marriage alive. As our children grew to adulthood, we also increased our get-away times. Due to my international travel keeping us frequently apart, we have now increased our get-aways to four times a year. This has become a priority for the two of us. Today at age 65, I rejoice with the wife of my youth!

Seasons of Marriage

DAY 2

"To everything there is a season, a time for every purpose under heaven" (Ecclesiastes 3:1). In marriage, as in any other relationship, this verse rings true. As Larry and I look back across our past 50 years together, we have experienced many different seasons in our relationship.

When I first met Larry, I was fully committed to the Lord, but he was a church member who lived much differently around me than he did when with his other friends. At age 18, Larry completely committed his life to Jesus Christ. We were both really passionate for God and became involved in Bible studies with our local youth group. Soon we began ministering to young teens in our community who needed to know the Lord. Our dating years were filled with ministry to kids both in our youth group and to unchurched youth in our local community. It was a good season.

All of these seasons include life issues, stressors that can affect our marriage relationships

During our courtship, our common desire to focus on our individual relationship with God and His corporate call on our lives set the tone for the success of our marriage. Marriage for the two of us began in our youth, I was 20 years of age and LaVerne was 19. After a short honeymoon we left for John's Island, South Carolina to serve as leaders of a Mennonite Mission called Voluntary Service. We lived on Johns Island off the coast of Charleston.

Larry worked with a construction team that tore down condemned buildings. His job was to remove the nails from the lumber and then repurpose the materials to build houses on the island for people who had very little or no money.

Although I barely knew how to sew, I hesitantly took leadership of a quilting club of older women. During this season, we worked with some amazing young leaders who were a part of our team that constantly looked for opportunities to share our faith in Christ.

At the time, Larry and I thought our marriage was doing quite well. Looking back, we now realize we had so much to learn, especially in the area of communication. If we had known back then, what we know now, it certainly would have saved us from repeated frustrations.

LaVerne had grown up in a home of outward processors who were much more verbal in communicating with each other than Larry had been accustomed to hearing. I grew up in a home of inward processors. My parents never had an argument in front of my sister and me. When LaVerne was quick to tell me her thoughts and opinions, I did not know how to respond. I felt devastated whenever her opinions differed from mine. I basically kept my reactions hidden, which really frustrated LaVerne. This difference in processing opened the door for a dark season in our marriage relationship.

After a year in Voluntary Service, LaVerne and I moved back to Pennsylvania. Larry worked with his father on the family farm. Both of us became involved in the youth ministry to unchurched youth that we had helped to start before becoming missionaries. With our dysfunctional communication patterns we actually came to the place where we felt we may have married the wrong person. We finally agreed to submit ourselves to a marriage counselor in hopes of saving our marriage. It was the best thing we could have done.

In the next season of marriage, we found ourselves raising small children and pastoring a church. As this church experienced tremendous growth, it eventually required training eight senior pastors and decentralizing one church into eight local congregations. It was the start of a family of churches. During one very difficult point, Larry became discouraged and wanted to quit all church leadership, which also had a negative effect upon our marriage. After Larry found hope and healing through being mentored by a more mature church leader, we entered a season of overseeing and training church leaders throughout many nations. We found this to be a much healthier season for us, but like each season previous to this one, it brought new and unexpected challenges to our marriage.

During this seasonal change of marriage we were apart more often due to Larry's international travel. Although I traveled with him occasionally, my primary role was to stay at home and care for our young children. Despite the frequent separations caused by the travel, we found ways to keep our marriage strong.

REFLECTION
Name some issues that you are facing in this season.

As our children grew to adulthood, we entered an all-new season, which included caring for our aging parents. Three of our parents passed away during this season. Today we are in another season.

Two of our four children are married and we have five grandchildren.

All of life's seasons include issues and stressors that affect marriage relationships. We've discovered that marriage brings a lot more difficult differences than arguments over which way the toothpaste is squeezed. LaVerne and I believe that acknowledging the hard parts of our marriage can be redemptive in helping readers learn from our experiences and recognize God's perspective.

Regardless of which season you are in today in your marriage relationship, we want to give you hope for your future. Do not waste your season. All things work together for good to those who love God (Romans 8:28).

Words Are Dynamite

DAY 3

When I was growing up, I thought beef liver looked and tasted disgusting, but when I got married, I discovered I had a beef-liver-loving wife! One day LaVerne prepared and served a beautiful meal. The meat smelled and tasted delicious. I asked, "Honey, what is this meat? It tastes exceptional."

LaVerne laughed and then to my utter surprise replied, "It's liver!"

Because LaVerne had seasoned the liver with the right seasonings, I really enjoyed it.

Our conversations can have the same effect. Words can be like dynamite. They can either be used powerfully for good, or they can be used powerfully for evil. Colossians 4:6 says, "Let your conversation be always full of grace, seasoned with salt, so that you may know how to answer everyone."

How can we speak to our spouse with grace, seasoned with salt?

If you feel like you need to share correction with your spouse to help him or her get back on the right course, season your speech with grace. In other words, say it in a way he or she can receive it. How we say it (with the right attitude and tone of voice) can be as important, if not more important, than the content of the message. Even a word of correction seasoned with grace can portray, "I care about you."

> There are some things that will never change about your wife.

We also often need to wait on God's timing to communicate some things to our spouse. There is a right and a wrong time to share correction with a spouse. A wise elderly counselor told me, "There are some things that will never change about your wife. Stop trying to change her."

While in Korea many years ago, I remembering hearing the mother-in-law of Dr. Paul Yonggi Cho, who was the pastor of the world's largest church, say, "We do not try to change the men in our lives, we just pray and let God push them around."

Her advice is sound advice for both husbands and wives. Let's spend more time praying for our spouses and less time trying to change them. Let God change them. Pick your battles wisely because many battles are not worth fighting.

The changes LaVerne and I have witnessed in our communication processes over the years are amazing to us. She no longer blurts out exactly what she feels at the moment as she did in our early years of our marriage. LaVerne says, "I have learned to set personal boundaries in the way I speak to my husband. I have learned to listen more and not jump to conclusions and judgments too quickly. Larry has learned the importance of waiting for the right time to talk to me about sensitive issues, and to pray for me rather than trying to change me. I have found that when I pray for Larry, he wants to change. God gives him the grace and the will to change."

The Bible tells us to speak the truth in love, so we may grow up in all things into Him who is the head—Christ (Ephesians 4:15). We must speak the truth, but it must be in love. And 1 Corinthians 13:4-7 tells us: "Love is patient and kind. Love is not jealous or boastful

REFLECTION

Have you learned to listen more and not jump to conclusions quickly?

or proud or rude. It does not demand its own way. It is not irritable, and it keeps no record of being wronged. It does not rejoice about injustice but rejoices whenever the truth wins out. Love never gives up, never loses faith, is always hopeful, and endures through every circumstance" (NLT).

Remember, it is not just what we say to our spouse that is important, but how and when we say it may be even more important.

Maintaining Proper Boundaries

DAY 4

After being married about four years, LaVerne and I experienced the most difficult time in our marriage. We were both deeply concerned that our marriage might not make it. We went to a Christian counselor for marriage counseling. He taught us the importance of having boundaries in our lives. That knowledge was life-changing.

God appoints limits and boundaries in our lives and he wants to us to keep them. In 2 Corinthians 10:13 we read, "We, however, will not boast beyond measure, but within the limits of the sphere which God appointed us."

> Establishing these boundaries together helped to save our lives.. and our marriage

Here is what was happening. I was getting up at 4:00 a.m. each day to go to work. Because we often had our house filled with new believers at night—sometimes staying at our house until after midnight—we were burning ourselves out. Our godly counselor told us that we needed to set proper boundaries and ask these young people to leave our home at a set time. This boundary provided time to be together as a family and time for much-needed sleep. Establishing these boundaries together helped us have healthy lives and a healthy marriage.

A second boundary we needed to set regarded giving counsel alone to those of the opposite sex. We felt they really needed us to help them, but we did not realize initially how we were becoming vulnerable. We read that Billy Graham set up a boundary in his life to keep himself from even the appearance of evil (1 Thessalonians 5:22). Billy would not spend time alone with any women other than his wife or his daughters. It was a boundary he believed the Lord gave to him. LaVerne and I learned after receiving counseling that we needed to do the same. We are so grateful the Lord gave us grace to set this boundary early in our marriage.

Consequently LaVerne does not worry that I am spending time with another woman while I travel and minister. I do not need to be questioning with whom she is spending time when I am not at home. Seldom do immoral relationships begin intentionally. Immoral relationships often start innocently. Sometimes it's simply someone showing an interest in us and connecting emotionally in a way that only our spouse should be connecting. Proper boundaries keep us safe in times of vulnerability. As modeled by Billy Graham, our desire is to finish well as we obey the Lord and keep the boundaries the Lord has appointed for us.

After I had became a pastor, LaVerne and I set another boundary—take a day off each week as a Sabbath day. Sunday is certainly no Sabbath day for LaVerne and I because it is filled with preaching, training leaders and spending time with people. Instead, Thursday is our designated "Sabbath." We turn off our phones on Thursdays and take a day off. It is a boundary that helps save our marriage.

A different kind of boundary is to know when a third party is needed to help solve marriage problems. We beg you, lay aside your pride and do not hesitate to get needed help. Reaching out to receive help for your marriage is strength, not weakness. Be real. Don't cover up your struggles; be authentic. Counseling can save your life and marriage.

Spouses also need to realize that most problems in marriage are much more of a personal issue than an actual marriage one. When each of us finds healing and wholeness personally, we will find

REFLECTION
Are you aware of needing to set boundaries in a particular area of your life?

hope and restoration in our marriage in a whole new way. A few years ago LaVerne and I went through the Restoring the Foundations ministry developed by Chester and Betsy

Kylstra[1]. We took the course that focuses on healing and freedom from life's deepest struggles because we wanted to be sure we are continuing to walk in wholeness both individually and as husband and wife. The majority of the ministry we received during those five days was individual, but we found our marriage relationship was refreshed and strengthened after this week of mostly personal ministry.

Our marriages need a regular checkup. We take our vehicles to the service station for a regular oil change and service checkup. Why not schedule a designated checkup on our marriages?

DAY 5
Love, Respect, Power of Encouragement

"Nevertheless let each one of you in particular so love his own wife as himself, and let the wife see that she respects her husband" (Ephesians 5:33).

A few years ago we discovered a secret to strengthen our marriage: the power of love and respect. Dr. Emerson Eggerichs made this concept popular in his book with the same title. I learned that if I truly love LaVerne, she will want to respect me. And LaVerne learned that if she truly respects me, I will love her. It is a win-win for our marriage relationships.

We have taught this truth to people in many parts of the world because it really works regardless of nationality.

When a husband practices truly loving his wife, he discovers that his wife finds it much easier to respect him. And vise versa. Much of the ability to respect and love depends on learning how to encourage one another.

There is such power released in encouragement. Hebrews 10:25 (NLT) tells us, "And let us not neglect our meeting together, as some people do, but encourage one another, especially now that the day of his return is drawing near." This need for encouragement is especially true in marriage.

Some years ago I was ministering in Hawaii. I noticed an elderly Japanese couple holding hands while sitting in the front row listening to me preach. It was very noticeable to me that she was literally

> Much of the ability to respect and love depends on learning how to encourage one another.

beaming. After the service was over, I asked them to tell me about themselves. The elderly Japanese man looked at his wife with admiration as he said, "She is my 'Empress.'" He saw her as a queen and she radiated with his love and affirmation. He had learned the power of encouragement.

In many African nations, the man needs to pay a dowry to the parents of his wife-to-be before they release her to him in marriage. The dowry is usually given in cows, not dollars. I heard the story about an ordinary young lady in a village who was asked by a young man to marry him.

Even though the dowry for her would have been only two or three cows, her fiancé gave her father fifty cows. She became known in the village as the 50-cow woman. She beamed from ear to ear. She felt transformed, valued and encouraged by her new husband.

The Bible tells us that a woman reflects man's glory (1 Corinthians 11:7). A Bible teacher once said he never makes a judgment on how he feels about a minister until he meets his wife because she is a reflection of her husband.

Many years ago, I (LaVerne) was impressed with the Scripture in Proverbs 20:5, "A plan in the heart of a man is like deep waters, but a man of understanding draws it out." This not only refers to an individual life, but I believe it is imperative in a marriage. I knew my encouragement, prayer and understanding of Larry's vision and heart would enable his potential to come forth.

Let's each make it a point to find ways to encourage our spouse daily by our words and by our actions. Sometimes what

REFLECTION

How do you encourage your spouse to feel valued?

is encouraging to us is not encouraging to our spouse. We need to discover what is most effective in helping our spouse to feel valued.

Honor Spouse's Love Language

DAY 6

Pastor and author Gary Chapman says that after thirty years as a marriage counselor, he is convinced there are five basic love languages—five ways to express love emotionally. Each person has a primary love language. We should use their love language when relating to them if we desire them to feel loved.

These five basic love languages include: words of affirmation, acts of service, receiving gifts, quality time and physical touch. We will explain each of these five basic love languages so you can determine you and your spouse's personal love language(s). Although many of us have two or three love languages, we each have a primary love language.

Let's start with words of affirmation. Last week while visiting our daughter and son-in-law and their family, he expressed how our daughter has been a positive influence on his life. Inwardly I rejoiced, "This is awesome!" because I knew the power of affirmation.

> We each have a primary love language.

I can't tell you how many men and women we have talked to who have either said or implied, "I work hard all day for our family, but I never get a single word of appreciation." If your spouse's primary love language is words of affirmation, your spoken praise and appreciation will make all of the difference to them. Before long, you will see vibrant life released in your marriage as your spouse responds to your words of love and encouragement.

Second: acts of service. We all remember the old saying: "Actions speak louder than words." For some spouses, that is particularly true of love. If "acts of service" is your spouse's primary love language, nothing will speak more deeply to him or her emotionally than finding ways to share simple acts of service like repairing something broken in the house, vacuuming or cooking a favorite meal

Some spouses think, "I'm sick of hearing 'I love you.' If he loved me, he would do something to help me." This person's primary love language is acts of service (not words of affirmation). Their spouse needs to learn to express love in a way that makes him or her feel valued.

Third: receiving gifts. Gift giving has always been perceived as an expression of love. Many of us believe that if you love someone, you will give a gift at least occasionally. For some people, receiving gifts is their primary love language. It's the thing that makes them feel loved most deeply. If you're married to someone whose primary love language is gift giving, you will make your spouse feel loved and treasured by giving gifts on birthdays, holidays, anniversaries and even better for "absolutely no reason but I love you" days. No need for expensive gifts, it's the thought that counts.

Fourth: quality time. If your spouse's love language is quality time, giving him or her your undivided attention is one of the best ways you can show your love. Turn off the TV, lay down the magazine, look into your mate's eyes, listen and interact. If quality time is your spouse's love language, a few minutes of your undivided attention—listening and conversing—is like a refill of his or her love tank.

Guys, if your wife's love language is quality time and you really want to impress her, the next time she walks into the room while you are watching sports, put the television on mute and don't take your eyes off your wife as long as she is in the room. Give her your undivided attention. You will score a thousand points!

Last, but not least, is number five: physical touch. We all know the emotional power of physical touch. Long before a baby understands the meaning of the word love, he or she feels loved by physical touch. In marriage, physical touch includes everything from putting a hand on your mate's shoulder, touching his or her leg as you're driving together, holding hands while you're walking, to kissing, embracing and sexual intercourse. If physical touch is your spouse's primary love language, nothing communicates love more clearly than for you to take the initiative to touch your mate.

The five love languages are the five different ways we say or express, "I love you." If you want to learn more about the five love languages, pick up the book *5 Love Languages*[1] by Gary Chapman and take the test to discover your love languages.

Ephesians 6:21 exhorts us to submit to one another in the fear of God. This happens practically as we honor our mate by taking the initiative to love them as we practice their own personal primary love languages. True biblical love is not merely a feeling but giving love with no expectancy of return. The feelings of love follow the actions of love.

REFLECTION

What is your spouse's love language?

DAY 7

Trying to Fix Your Spouse "Ain't Gonna Work"

Jesus tells us in Luke 6:41, "And why do you look at the speck in your brother's eye, but do not perceive the plank in your own eye?"

Your brother in this verse refers to someone close to you. It wasn't long after we had married that I began to realize that the woman I had married was not perfect. I tried to change her to become more like me because I thought that I had my act together and could certainly help her do the same.

Additionally, I could not understand why LaVerne was so emotional at times. She wanted to discuss how she felt about life situations. I believed she should learn to stand on the Word of God regardless of how she felt. The plank of pride in my eye was so big that it blinded me from giving my wife the help she needed.

Whenever LaVerne began to talk about how she really felt, my mind began to race toward the most appropriate scripture in order to fix her. One day she told me, "I do not need to hear you give me another scripture, and I do not need you to fix me. I just want you to listen to me!" Eventually I learned to listen instead of preach at LaVerne. It made a huge difference. I found that when I truly listened to her, I was able to validate her thoughts and emotions. That enabled her to trust God and find freedom because the Holy Spirit spoke to her without me quoting scriptures to fix her.

I also could not understand why LaVerne seemed so emotional at times. Eventually it dawned on me that I really do not understand how women think and feel. I was told about a newly published book, *Everything Men Know About Women.*[1] It was a really thick book, but when it was opened, the pages were all blank! I found this to be realistic for me as I was basically clueless.

> "I do not need to hear you give me another scripture, and I do not need you to fix me.

Today, I have a deep respect and appreciation for La-Verne. For example, she can walk into a room full of people and have a sense that something is not right. I cannot seem to pick up on these kinds of intuitions, but I have learned to trust hers. She often sees and senses things that I miss. The worse thing would be for me to expect her to be like me because together we complement one another. I love that we are different.

The older we get, the more we see God's hand of blessing on our lives. Together, we desire to help younger generations find this same blessing for their marriages and to stop trying to fix one another.

I (LaVerne) have learned to truly honor and appreciate how the Lord has wired Larry. I am no longer tempted to just tolerate the differences in our personalities, but I value him and the perspective that he brings into our lives and marriage. We both love what author Gary Thomas asks in his book *Sacred Marriage*, "What if God designed marriage to make us holy more than to make us happy?"

The Scriptures tell us to walk in the light. Ephesians 5:8 says it clearly, "For you were once darkness, but now you are light in the Lord. Walk as children of light."

REFLECTION

Are you trying to fix your spouse?

You cannot fix your spouse, but you can be truthful; walk in the light and live a life of transparency. Expect the Lord to do something fresh and new in your marriage relationship. But remember, trying to fix your spouse is not recommended.

CHAPTER 2

Marriage: What Was God Thinking!

Steve and Mary Prokopchak

Marriage: Creation Act of God

DAY 1

Marriage did not begin as a Christian concept. Does that statement surprise you?

It shouldn't and here's why: Marriage actually predates Christianity because it was God's design from the beginning of the world, a creation act of God. According to Genesis 2, our heavenly Father created marriage and called it "good" when He brought one man to one woman and pronounced them husband and wife.

We love that God's Son affirms this act of God's creation for us as Christ followers today. In Mark 10:6–8, Jesus said, "But at the beginning of creation God made them male and female. For this reason a man will leave his father and mother and be united to his wife and the two will become one flesh."

> Each husband and wife team must recognize that marriage is not about *me*, but rather, *us*.

Each husband and wife team must recognize that marriage is not about *me*, but rather, *us*. It's the Philippians 2 principle: "Being one in spirit and purpose. Do nothing out of selfish ambition or vain conceit, but in humility consider others (my spouse) better than yourselves. Each of you should look not only to your own interests, but also to the interests of others" (Philippians 2: 2-4). Maturity says, "I want to serve my mate and make sure his or her needs are met first." Immaturity is the attitude: "I want what I want when I want it."

For that reason, Mary and I encourage singles not to seek marriage, but rather, seek maturity. When two mature persons come together as one, there is a far greater chance of marital unity and commitment. When two immature persons marry, they often expect the spouse to fulfill all their needs, which does not happen.

In God's divine wisdom, He often gives a spouse who is strong in areas where the other spouse is weak, someone to partner with us in life and someone with whom we can become one.

Examine yourself: Are you becoming "better?" Are you pursuing wholeness to become what your life mate needs?

Gary Thomas, author of the book, *Sacred Marriage*[1], says that spouses are each other's mirrors. What are you reflecting back to your mate?

REFLECTION

If you are each other's mirrors, what are you reflecting back to your mate?

Early in our marriage Mary and I did not understand the "oneness" principle. At times we'd say something such as "how could I be so stupid?" Although we did not criticize each other, we didn't mind saying something negative about ourselves. One day we realized that according to the oneness principle, Steve is Mary and Mary is Steve. If Steve puts Steve down, Steve is also putting Mary down and vice versa. That, we discovered, was wrong and a weak spot in our divine call.

No perfect marriage exists because no person is perfect. Marriage issues result from two imperfect persons.

Although our marriages are not perfect, we do serve the Perfect One—the author of marriage.

Freedom of Submission

Every marriage is a "broken" marriage, because each of us is broken and we marry into brokenness. Broken people are in need of healing and maturity.

Getting married changes our status but not our life issues. In fact, life issues can actually be accentuated by marriage. Your wife can bring the worst out of you and you her. How can that change? It changes through a spirit of submission and honor. Let us explain.

Ephesians 5:21 says, "Submit one to another out of reverence for Christ." The book of Romans tells us to, "Honor one another above yourselves" (Romans 12:10). When we submit to Christ, we are saying, "not my will but His be done." We honor Him by obeying His voice and His command. We know He will not ask us to do something that will harm or hurt us. We trust Him and His Word. But do we trust Him enough to obey Him in honoring or submitting to our spouse out of a position of love and respect?

The Greek word for submission is *hupotasso*, which means, "to arrange under." It was used as a military term to signify that the army was arranged under the leadership of another leader. The army trusted its leader (sometimes blindly) to lead them into battle and win the battle, which resulted in a lot of self-sacrificing and laying down of the soldiers' lives. Unless soldiers deserted the ranks, they moved forward as one, fulfilling the mission.

Marriage is similar. Submitting to one another in honor is a key position for each spouse to humbly choose. It is saying that I am not in a position in which I am better than you. Although we are different and not the same, we are equal in our value before God (see Galatians 3:28). It is important to understand this concept before we examine Ephesians 5:22, one of the most misunderstood and controversial verses in the Bible.

Ephesians 5:22 also incorporates the submission word and states, "Wives, submit to your husbands as to the Lord." The same Greek word *hupotasso*—to arrange under—is used in verse twenty-one. Many years ago Mary and I asked God to show us what this scripture meant and what might be a picture to help us understand it. God was faithful to answer us. We believe what He showed us can bring tremendous freedom to each marriage.

> Getting married changes our status but not our life issues.

The picture is that of a long bridge over a wide river. The first step in building this bridge is digging deep below the surface of the water and pouring concrete pillars that eventually support the bridge surface. Later the bridge surface is bolted onto the pillars through the use of long steel girders. Eventually cars and trucks safely drive over the concrete surface of the bridge.

Question: Which is more important, the pillars or the actual bridge surface? While the pillars provide the support structure, travel across the bridge is not possible without a concrete surface. The bridge surface is what everyone sees and admires; but without the pillars sitting on bedrock, the bridge will eventually collapse into the river.

Both are equally important; you cannot have one without the other. By working together, they complete the mission. When we take another look at the English word submission, we see the prefix—*sub*. Sub means "under," as in submarine or subsurface. Just like the army, the Bible is saying that wives are to come under. However this verse is not saying as a lesser under the husband, but under the mission. In the end, the question that needs to be addressed is "Husbands, what is the mission?"

If husbands do not define the mission, wives will not understand to what they are to submit. This scripture is not suggesting that men can ask or force their wives to do whatever their hearts desire in the name of submission. Instead it is requiring husbands to define the mission of marriage.

REFLECTION
Do we trust God enough to obey Him in submitting to our spouse out of a position of love and respect?

Marriage With a Mission

DAY 3

Why are we married, where are we going and what is the purpose of this thing called marriage?

Submission is a wonderful word because mission is at the heart of it. It is the safety and the affirmation of coming under a mission, a direction for marriage and family. It is saying husbands and wives are called together to fulfill something—our call from God. Do you have a business? Then you have a mission. Do you lead a small group as a couple? Then you have a mission. Are you training children together? That mission is evident and extremely important.

God gave Adam and Eve, the first couple, a mission. He said to tend the garden and fill the earth with children. When God sent His Son to earth, He gave Him a mission. And from the cross Jesus said, "It is finished." Christ gave us the great commission in which we are to go to the entire world with the gospel. The Apostle Paul said it was his mission to see Christ formed in his disciples (Galatians 4:19 and Colossians 1:28).

> Spiritual intimacy will not occur unless both individuals put the needs of the spouse before their own needs.

If you as a couple are not clear on the mission, you'll never be clear on mutual submission. Couples with mission statements are stronger couples. When children know their parents have a mission, a direction, they are more secure in their family. A marriage mission statement creates purpose and goals; but more importantly, values. It reveals to us who we are becoming one. It's like super glue holding us together for a united single-mindedness. A clear mission will help to keep us on track morally, spiritually, financially and directionally. It helps us identify what we need to change to remain strong as a couple and as a family. More than anything, when we define our mission, we concurrently define submission to our wives and families.

Marriage mission statements envision a future. Where do you desire to be as a couple in a year or five years? Our mission should include short- and long-term goals toward a healthier and more fulfilling future. Your local church most likely has a mission statement, as does your workplace. Why shouldn't your marriage have a paragraph that describes the purpose of who you are as a couple and where you are going?

Let's build a marriage mission statement together.

1. **List areas** that you and your spouse are presently prioritizing and involved in individually and as a couple. (This may include raising a family, jobs, ministry, paying for your house, politics or coaching sports, caring for extended family, and so forth).

2. **Take the time to list your values.** Your values are the most important things in your life. They are the practical things that define your marriage. (For example: praying together; desiring to live debt free or desiring to protect each another.)

3. **Start building your mission statement** by listing your goals and dreams, utilizing what you wrote above. What do you desire to accomplish as a married couple? Include both short- and long-term dreams and vision. Think spiritually, physically, financially, socially, vocationally and recreationally. Answer the question: "What impact do we desire to make as a couple?"

    Example: *To love and to serve God: to love, to serve and to complement one another in order to see the purposes of God fulfilled in our spouse's life; to raise our children in the truth of God's Word—training them in the way they should go; to be people helpers in the body of Christ —through counseling, consulting, teaching, volunteering, and so forth; and to become debt free.*

4. **From this statement, what are short- and long-term goals** that will help us to fulfill our cooperative mission statement together?

    Goal #1

    Goal #2

    Goal #3

Skill of Listening

People pay therapists $150 per hour to have someone listen to them. Actually that price does not cover a full hour, more like 50 minutes. After 50 minutes of hearing responses such as, "Yes, I see," and "how did that make you feel?" the counselee feels better. How does that happen? The therapist listened—really listened—to the hurting wife. Secretly she often wishes her husband was like the therapist.

Listening is a developed skill. It says to the one speaking, "You are important enough for all of my attention." The therapist responds appropriately (because he has been listening) and doesn't have his newspaper, phone or computer in his hand. In fact, he is taking notes from the conversation so he can remember what was said. Can you imagine—in your wildest dreams—of having your spouse take notes on your conversation?

> When listening, ask appropriate questions for clarity and feedback.

Are you a good listener or are you too distracted to really listen? Public speaking courses are offered in high schools and colleges across the country, but when have you heard of a public listening course being offered? Listening means you do not interrupt the speaker but concentrate on what you are being told. Here are some listening guidelines:

- When listening, give good eye contact and nonverbal nods.

- When listening, eliminate as many distractions as possible. (Put the phone down; turn off the TV).

- Stop thinking about your response; concentrate on listening.

- When necessary and needful, repeat what you hear so you are sure you have heard correctly.

- When listening, ask appropriate questions for clarity and feedback.

Effective listening adds value to the one speaking. Proverbs 18:13 tells us, "He who answers before listening—that is his folly and his shame." James 1:19 reveals, "Everyone should be quick to listen, slow to speak and slow to become angry." Imagine a customer service person that does not have the ability to listen to the customer, or a judge who refuses to hear your side of the story.

If the one sending the message desires a response from you, hear the whole story before responding.

One evening after a long day of counseling Steve returned home and engaged in a conversation with me. I talked about my day and about a conversation I had with someone I had met. Repeatedly Steve interrupted me to tell me that I should have said something different or responded in a "better" way (his way). I started crying and retorted, "Oh, you're the great counselor!"

I didn't think I deserved that comment. After all, I had been actively listening to my wife despite my exhaustion after a long day at work.

But Mary was right. I had not removed my counseling hat and was still in my Mr. Fix-it mode. Mary did not need me to "fix" her; she needed me to listen. Since that confrontational moment, I have learned to adapt and add this question to our discussions, "Do you want me to listen or do you want my response/input?" That question defuses a lot of misinterpreted dialogue.

REFLECTION
Do you give good eye contact and nonverbal nods while listening to your spouse?

One day I saw this sign posted at the bank: "We do not have tellers, only listeners." That is a great message if followed through.

Fight, Argue or Pray, Agree

DAY 5

Early in our marriage, while serving in a full-time missions organization, we came to a bit of a revelation. When it came to conflict, we could choose to "fight and argue" or we could "pray and agree." Disagreement is powerful, but even more powerful is agreement. The scriptures tell us that if any two persons will **agree** together in prayer they will receive what they have asked (Matthew 18:19).

Here's a personal illustration of this concept: our most frequent disagreements centered on our personal views of finances because Mary was a "spender" and Steve was a "saver." Those two opposing values often clashed. Both values had positives and negatives. Mary and I had to move beyond disagreement of right and wrong to prayer by asking for God's direction and discernment.

A scriptural precedent that really helped us is James 3, which addresses two types of wisdom: earthly and heavenly. Earthly wisdom can be full of selfish ambition, but heavenly wisdom is peace loving and submissive, full of mercy. James 4:1 asks where do fights and quarrels come from? The

> Both values had positivies and negatives.

scripture reveals that the core of disagreement is because we want something but are not getting it. In other words, Steve wants one thing, but Mary wants another. We might both desire something good. However, the answer James gives is that we should ask God without selfish motives, rather than demand our desires from each other.

Mary and I discovered that if we sought the Lord first, He enabled us to see our partner's view more quickly. God helped us to move toward wanting to bless the other rather than withhold and remain selfish. He helped us to see that our use of the terms "spender" and "saver" were terms of critical judgment and negative attitudes toward the other. God gave us new language: Mary was actually a "giver" and Steve was actually a "planner/investor" for future needs.

It's natural to have disagreements at times. It would be unnatural not to have any disagreements. When we deeply love someone or care about someone, our disagreements can be even more intense because we have so much invested in the relationship. We each have our perspective, our filters and our view through the lens of our histories, experiences, life training, families of origin, and fears. Disagreement in a relationship is not the problem, staying in the mode of disagreement or fighting is a problem. We must stop long enough to discern what it is we need and find the solution(s) to reach agreement toward those need(s).

Strive to set aside the intensity of the disagreement and focus on the following five questions:

1. **What are you feeling?** Describe your feelings, not just your thoughts.

2. **What do you need?** Describe your desired need or desired outcome.

3. **What do you understand?** Share with your mate what you are hearing from them about their feelings and their needs.

REFLECTION

Do you fight and argue or pray and agree?

4. **What have you tried?** This step helps you to figure out what hasn't worked.

5. **What are the solutions?** Move all of the above toward a solution, a plan to resolve the difference. Look for a healthy solution and action plan with which you both can accept.

Most Intimate Marriage Act

Sex is not the most intimate act in which two persons can be involved. In fact, two persons can be sexual but not intimate. Mary and I believe and teach that prayer is the most intimate action in which couples can participate.

Many couples forfeit praying together. Instead a spouse may pray with a friend on a regular basis. Nothing is wrong with having a prayer partner, but to exclude praying with our spouse is to exclude them from a deep and intimate connection. When spouses pray together, they reveal their hearts to one another. Perhaps that's why many couples today do not pray together. We must pray out of relationship **for** one another not **at** one another. In order to do this, the place of prayer must be a safe place. Our spouse needs to allow us to open up and be real while describing our feelings to God. If we do not feel safe with each other, we will not disclose our heart.

> If we do not feel safe with each other, we will not disclose our heart.

Earlier we wrote that James 4 begins with a question by asking the source of fights and quarrels among us. James, with Holy Spirit inspiration, states that they come from desires that battle within us. We want something but we're not getting it. Think of any recent conflict, and you will discover that you wanted one thing and your mate desired another. The conclusion, then, is to stop arguing, demanding and fighting and start praying—asking God. When we ask God, we are not to ask selfishly, but for the good of others.

During those eight years of mission work, Mary and I served "by faith." There was very little financial compensation other than food and housing. We still had the expense of monthly personal needs and payments. The funds to pay these came as we prayed and agreed together. Thus we learned that we had two options: fight and argue or pray and agree. The latter is far more life giving and relationship building. It actually forces us to see God as our provider rather than demanding ongoing provision from our spouse.

God was faithful. For eight years Mary and I prayed in agreement, and for eight years, God provided what we needed and sometimes what we wanted. The lessons we learned in those days of dependence on Him have stayed with us during the following 32 years. There is power in agreement and there is power in prayer. Together they open up a whole new world of faith in the One who is faithful.

The following are additional areas to keep in mind as you learn to pray together:

- Learn to pray at each other's level, rather than praying beyond our mate. In other words, don't try to be more spiritual than your spouse during your prayer time.
- Make prayer together a place that is nonjudgmental—a place where we are able to share openly without feeling judged or criticized.

- Prayer is the place to release our hopes and dreams to God before our mate—and not just about needs and wants.

- Prayer is an intimate place of listening to God and listening to our spouse.

- Prayer is a place of worship with our spouse.

- Prayer is the place to release anxiety to the Lord. We learn that we have a choice to either worry and fret over our needs or pray (Philippians 4: 6, 7).

Here are some examples of times to pray:

- At mealtime

- Before leaving for work or school

- In the evening upon completing your day or after putting the kids to bed

- Early Saturday morning before the kids are awake

- While driving in the car together

- While walking around the neighborhood

Amos 3:3 states, "Do two walk together unless they have agreed to do so?" Prayer is the most intimate thing we can have as we walk together. Do not let the enemy steal it from you or rob you from this intimacy. It takes courage to be committed to praying together.

REFLECTION

When is the best time of the day and where is the best place to connect for a time of prayer together?

Three Most Powerful Sentences

Three sentences have transformed my wife's and my ability to move on and forgive one another in order to achieve a long-term marriage. These sentences have helped us to lay aside our personal agenda and humble ourselves.

What are these sentences? *I am sorry; I was wrong; please forgive me.* Most of us find it rather easy to use those sentences when apologizing for bumping into a complete stranger. However, when our spouse "bumps" into us (such as giving us the cold shoulder or answering with one or two words rather than with meaningful conversation), we are not as eager to use those sentences. Instead we question our spouse's motives. How can we instantaneously forgive a stranger, but when it comes to the one we love most on this earth—not even offer the benefit of the doubt?

> We want something but we're not getting it.

Here's the difference. We have far more invested in our marriage relationship. We are far more committed, emotionally attached to and have a sense of deep love for our spouse. We experience none of those feelings with a total stranger. We have nothing invested in that relationship. To apologize to them is almost meaningless and easily done with no emotion connected.

The primary human issue that gets in the way is pride, which blocks our willingness to forgive. Pride wants to be right. Pride keeps us from being willing to start the conversation toward healing. Pride keeps our mouth shut and our heart aching. Proverbs 8:13 states that God hates pride. Pride precedes destruction or a fall (Proverbs 16:18).

The book of Daniel in the Bible describes how the Lord dealt with Nebuchadnezzar's pride. "Those who walk in pride he is able to humble" (Daniel 4:37).

Do you want to be right or do you want to be in relationship? That's a thought-provoking question because it requires us to make a choice: either our relationship is more important or our pride in being right and saving face. Pride will kill relationships slowly. It will keep us in a defensive mode. If we are not careful, we become offended, causing wounds to become even deeper.

Proverbs 18:19 sheds light on the area of offenses when it says, "An offended brother is more unyielding than a fortified city." In addition, Scripture reminds us that when we overlook an offense, we promote love (Proverbs 17:9).

REFLECTION

Do I want to be right or do I want to be in relationship?

When you are wrong—admit it. When you know it's your responsibility to initiate forgiveness, start by saying, *"I am sorry; I was wrong; or please forgive me.* Allow those words if needed to become part of your conversation before bedtime. Do not go to bed angry

(Ephesians 4:26-27). Whenever needed, use those sentences as soon as possible. Those sentences will help to keep you moving forward without remaining stuck in an ongoing argument. Teach your children those sentences and share them with others you love.

Repeat those sentences until they become instinctive to say. Give your life mate the benefit of the doubt even when you are positively convinced yours is the correct viewpoint. Recognize that perhaps your attitude was not without fault.

CHAPTER 3

Under the Covers

Duane and Reyna Britton

In the Beginning

"In the beginning God created the heavens and the earth."

Genesis 1 reveals that God continues creating His world: light, water, vegetation, animals, birds. . . . Verse 31 states, "Then God looked over all he had made, and he saw that it was very good!" What a pronounced statement summing up His six days of work. In Genesis 2:18 (NLT), God makes a startling statement. God saw something in His creation that wasn't good. He said, "It is not good for the man to be alone."

What was not good about a perfect place with the perfect creation of living things? Adam had everything and could access anything he wanted, but God knew that Adam wouldn't be fulfilled. God knew that man would need intimacy—relationship with another individual.

God created man with emotional, physical, intellectual and spiritual needs. Even though Adam experienced intimacy with God—walking with God in the Garden—God knew that a God-man relationship alone could not fulfill Adam's every need. So God said, "I will make a helper who is just right for him." Human beings were never meant to live a hermit, loner, solitary life. Nor are they intended to be self-sufficient.

God created woman out of Adam's rib to be the significant part or aspect of him. The nature—essence of the woman—was to be different from that of man. God created two sexes. The scriptures, social research, biological and psychological scientific data all confirm the fact that men and women are not the same. They are different but like two pieces of a puzzle that fit together resulting in an expansion and multiplication of themselves.

We were created for intimacy—not just sexual intimacy but complete intimacy. Intimacy is having a powerfully close connection with another. This involves every

> The nature–essence of the woman—was to be different from that of man...

aspect of an individual whether emotional, intellectual, physical or spiritual. It is having detailed knowledge of the other person in all these areas and bonding with them. Consequently in our marriage relationships, we really need to evaluate how well we know each other and are bonded together.

How well do you know your spouse in these four areas of intimacy? It is important to review your relationship with each other in order to determine how well you are doing in these key aspects of intimacy. Marriage, by God's intention, is to be the most mutually enjoyable and intimate relationship that humans experience while on this earth. It is designed and envisioned to be more intimate than a father-son relationship, mother-daughter relationship, and parent-child or boyfriend-girlfriend relationship. A couple's friendship should embody the inordinate level of intimacy God created us to attain and experience.

How can we get closer? Closeness occurs when both husband and wife become vulnerable, trusting and transparent with each other. It is experienced through sharing one's life, thoughts, joys, fears, dreams and concerns with each other. Developing deeper levels of intimacy takes time, effort and discipline. It is a life-long process. It is so easy to get sidetracked as life gets busy with work demands, children, household chores, hobbies and the many "other" good things that can take time away from being with and knowing our life mate on a deeper level.

To help cultivate their friendship, we encourage couples to set aside time regularly to share and listen to one other, even if it's only several minutes a day. Think about how people develop friendship. They spend time together. They do life together and through those interactions and conversations they get to know each other on a deeper level. Their relationship becomes a priority in each other's life.

"Marriage is the highest state of friendship. If happy, it lessens our cares by dividing them, at the same time that it doubles our pleasures by mutual participation" — Samuel Richardson (*BrainyQuote.Com*).

REFLECTION
Do you and your spouse share intimacy emotionally, intellectually, physically and spiritually?

Wow...Are We Different!

What does intimacy means to you? If you ask any group of couples that question, you will likely receive a variety of answers. One definition that we have heard over the years is that intimacy actually means "*In-To-Me-See.*" Intimacy is the ability to see into each other's lives in a way that you will know each other's strengths and weaknesses, as well as each other's fears, dreams and hopes.

It is no surprise that God has wired women and men differently. We all recognize some of these unique differences, but others often hide in plain sight. Differences as spouses tend to hinder our abilities to become more intimate because we do not fully understand or know how to adjust to each other. The truth is that men and women are different! Understanding these differences will help us know each other on a deeper level, which in turn leads to greater intimacy.

> One definition that we have heard over the years is that intimacy actually means "In-To-Me-See.".

Before we look at some of the differences between men and women, let's consider the following qualifications. These differences are generalizations; they aren't judgments. They're generalized differences between the sexes that God creatively designed to help men and women be better partners such as the following:

- Women want emotional connection in their friendships. Men look to their friends for camaraderie.

- Women tend to affirm their identity in forming close relations, while men gain their identity through vocations.

- When women need encouragement, they want hugs from their supportive friends. Men typically go for the slap on the back from the guys on the court for encouragement.

- Women think of intimacy in emotional terms (T-A-L-K). Men think of intimacy in physical terms (S-E-X).

When you see these differences demonstrated, realize that God created both men and women differently to fulfill His expressed purposes. God knew what we would need from each other. When He designed us He knew what He was doing.

"It is not good for the man to alone; I will make him a helper [a completer] suitable for him" (Genesis 2:18).

God has an intended framework for the relationship between a man and a woman. Every part of our identities will be affected by how we live out that design.

Our failure to recognize and appreciate these differences can become a life-long source of disappointment, frustration, tension and eventually could lead to the downfall of the relationship. Problems simply arise when we expect or assume the opposite sex should think, feel or act the way we do. Rather than being frustrated by gender differences, decide to respect them and learn how to work with them instead of against them.

An essential ingredient of intimacy is allowing your spouse to be himself or herself without striving to conform to your ideals. In intimacy, we try to grow closer together, not to eliminate the "otherness" but to enjoy each other's differences.

The opposite of self-centeredness is love. Love will concentrate on the well-being of the other, meaning we take time to listen and understand the thoughts, feelings and desires of our spouse. Paul writes in 1 Corinthians 13:4-7 [GNT], "Love is patient and kind; it is not jealous or conceited or proud; love is not ill-mannered or selfish or irritable; love does not keep a record of wrongs; love is not happy with evil, but is happy with the truth. Love never gives up; and its faith, hope, and patience never fail."

REFLECTION
How do you allow your spouse to be himself or herself without striving to conform to your ideals?

In loving, we seek to understand and choose to become supportive and caring for each other. The reality is that we are different but we must not, even with good intentions, seek to undermine those differences.

Spiritual Intimacy

DAY 3

"Two are better than one because they have a good return for their hard work" (Ecclesiastes 4:9).

Spiritual intimacy in marriage requires more than spending time together reading God's Word. It's about learning how to connect with your spouse through your faith. Often times, couples say they *"can't connect with their spouse"* because they're not in the same place spiritually.

H. Norman Wright wrote in *Developing Spiritual Intimacy in Marriage*, "Many marriage partners today feel close to their spouses in every way except spiritually. In that area they feel isolated. Often this isolation cannot be kept in check, and it may creep into other areas of a couples' life and impact those areas, too. And the more one person wants to be close spiritually and the other resists, the more resentment will build."[1]

> Spiritual intimacy will not occur unless both spouses put the needs of their spouse before their own needs.

If you're going to experience spiritual intimacy in your marriage, you must invest in spiritual intimacy. In reality, both spouses need the prayers and encouragement from each other. As you share spiritual experiences, you will become increasingly united in your thoughts, attitudes and goals.

We all have spiritual struggles from time-to-time and need the support of other members in the body of Christ. But a husband and wife have a unique relationship to support and encourage each other because of their covenant relationship.

The Preacher of Ecclesiastes writes that "two are better than one." Ecclesiastes 4:10-12 [CEB], "If either should fall, one can pick up the other. But how miserable are those who fall and don't have a companion to help them up! Also, if two lie down together, they can stay warm. But how can anyone stay warm alone? Also, one can be overpowered, but two together can put up resistance. A three-ply cord doesn't easily snap. Together they have more resources and can contribute to each other's lives."

Spiritual intimacy is a sense of unity and mutually submitted commitment to God's purpose for their lives and marriage coupled with a respect for the special dreams within each other's hearts. It's the greatest depth of intimacy that couples experience in marriage. Spiritual intimacy will not occur unless both spouses put the needs of the spouse before their own needs.

A godly marriage happens when two people created in God's image join together to help each other fulfill God's calls on their lives. When they value each other spiritually, they partner with God to help their spouse reach full spiritual potential.

You can start building intimacy in your spiritual life by praying daily for and with your spouse. Pray for greater depth in your relationship as a couple. Set aside a few minutes each day to go together before God with prayers for your marriage and blessing each other. If your spouse is not very spiritually motivated, keep your prayers short and do them at meal time or another non-intimidating time, such as praying for safe enjoyable travel while you are in the car together.

If you and your spouse aren't connecting around church, don't set high expectations for your spouse to attend church with you every Sunday. Start gradually. Don't set the bar so high that you're doomed to failure. Remember: small steps along the way make a big difference down the road.

Don't short change yourself or your spouse by not focusing on spiritual intimacy. Spiritual growth and intimacy is a growth process that requires time and commitment.

REFLECTION

How do you short change yourself or your spouse by not focusing on spiritual intimacy?

If you're going to experience spiritual intimacy in your marriage, you must invest in it. Value God's purposes for your spouse, pursue God together, sacrifice your own needs and desires, and create a safe, inviting atmosphere where you can help your husband or wife fulfill their dreams.

Going Under the Covers

DAY 4

"The husband should fulfill his wife's sexual needs, and the wife should fulfill her husband's needs" (1 Corinthians 7:3 NLT).

Sexuality is a sacred and *wonder-full* reflection of God. The Bible provides marriage advice on sexual relations that is timeless. Despite all that our present-day culture wants us to believe, research continually reveals that the most satisfying sexual relationships are those engaged in life-long monogamous married relationships. Physical intimacy is not the catalyst of marriage, but rather the continual culmination, and it is in this sense it is to be cherished and celebrated.

We've been wired by God with a sex drive that is one of the most powerful forces we can experience. However, like fire, when it is not contained and controlled, it becomes a damaging and destructive force. Physical intimacy in marriage is meant for mutual pleasure and to satisfy natural sensual desires. Our physical intimacy is a wonderful, sacred and good (blameless) thing.

Many are surprised to discover that one of the world's best examples of ancient erotic literature is in the Bible, the Song of Solomon. This book is rich in symbolism and figurative speech, and is filled with sexual references found in romantic love letters between a young husband and wife. Though the images may seem humorously distant from today's culture and languages of love, the verses are beautiful expressions of the sensual pleasure found in the romantic, erotic, physical intimacy of marriage

> We've been wired by God with a sex drive that is one of the most powerful forces we can experience.

God created us with physical senses and extraordinary capability to enjoy sex. Its first purpose as a gift of God is for reproduction and the second is for intimate union. The capacity for intimacy within a couple's relationship intensifies pleasure and oneness. Genesis 2:24 (NLT) says, "For this reason a man will leave his father and mother and be united to his wife, and they will become one flesh."

When the writer said that the man and woman become "one flesh," he was referring directly to sex. This is supported by 1 Corinthian 6:16 that states that a man who has sex with a prostitute becomes "one flesh" with her. The sexual act was meant to be a symbol of unity and intimacy in marriage, which is to be consistently cultivated. Sex must be enjoyed with propriety—mutual respect and it must be within the boundaries of marriage.

Proverbs 5:15-19 teaches the dangers of promiscuity as compared to the sacred beauty of sex within marriage. Sexual intimacy must be out of love and not lust and is the interactive process between husband and wife responding to passion for the other.

In 1 Corinthians 7:1-7 Paul cautions married couples against abstaining from sexual intimacy unless it is by mutual consent for the purpose of prayer and fasting and only for a short time. If we are not careful, we can contribute to each other's vulnerability to sexual temptations. Apostle Paul is not encouraging some sort of obligation that lends either spouse to being used or abused. His very point is a call for mutuality. In 1 Corinthians 7:3 (NLT) it reads, "The husband should fulfill his wife's sexual needs, and the wife should fulfill her husband's needs." We should never use physical intimacy as a weapon.

REFLECTION
Do you use physical intimacy as a weapon?

Sex is a celebratory gift that God created to enrich marriage. It is where intimacy and unity are cultivated, where the miracle of procreation happens, and where pure joy is stimulated and satisfied. However, it is also an all too common area where Satan attacks. Couples must guard against desecration of their sacred gift and cultivate it to be able to grow in intimacy with one another. Physical intimacy should be valued and enjoyed on a regular basis.

Sex–Get a Head Start

DAY 5

"Honor marriage, and guard the sacredness of sexual intimacy between wife and husband" (Hebrews 13:4).

Emily tries repeatedly over time to generate romantic thoughts for her husband Jarrod, but finds it extremely difficult. She intentionally makes plans earlier in the day that she will put her best effort forward to initiate physical intimacy that evening. She envisions herself making foreplay advances that cause her engines to get revived up, with Jarrod easily responding.

When it comes time to go to bed, even when the opportunity is ripe, she can't seem to follow through with what she had envisioned. At age 32, her sexual desires seem to be numbed and depleted. Something has to be done. She reasons that it isn't fair to Jarrod. It isn't how she wants things to be as they begin their seventh year of marriage.

During a lunch conversation with a friend, Emily shares that Jarrod has put on quite a bit of weight and that he comes home from work only to spend time in the garage restoring the classic car that his dad gave him. She continues to talk about the things that Jarrod does that annoy her. She realizes that her thoughts about Jarrod have shifted from him being the man that she loves, admires and respects to him being, in many ways, a source of irritation.

> They moved beyond a hurdle that deters quite a number of couples.

Emily has neglected the "thinking part" of love. Philippians 4:8 (NLT) instructs, "And now, dear brothers and sisters, one final thing. Fix your thoughts on what is true, and honorable, and right, and pure, and lovely, and admirable. Think about things that are excellent and worthy of praise."

Emily was having difficulty in initiating foreplay and finding Jarrod sexually desirable because one of her main sex organs—her brain, was counteracting her sexual desires and short-circuiting the cascade of physiological responses that contribute to sexual arousal and drive. Her thoughts tended to be negative or critical of Jarrod. They deterred her from engaging in thoughts that create pleasure, respect, desire, giving of herself and blessing him. Through her transparent conversation with her friend, Emily realized that her judgmental thoughts toward Jarrod needed to change.

Afterward she prayed and asked the Lord to forgive her and to restore her love, admiration and desire for Jarrod. She then shared with Jarrod how she had become critical of him and what negative effect it had on her. Her honesty led to them having an open conversation about their sexual desires. They moved beyond a hurdle that deters quite a number of couples. Couples should not fall short of exploring and removing any barrier that prevents them from achieving that satisfaction.

REFLECTION

How do judgmental thoughts toward each other affect your sex life?

Many factors lead to the capacity to enjoy satisfying sexual intimacy and fulfillment. For both spouses emotional, physical, intellectual knowledge and mental aspects of their lives contribute to their ability (or not) to enjoy mutually satisfying sexual intimacy with each other. It takes humility, determination, transparency, occasionally seeking expert/professional advisement, love and a commitment to each other throughout the entire marriage to maintain active sexual intimacy. It can be done even with couples who are married more than 60 years. We have personally heard and been inspired by a few testimonies of couples that have done so.

Paradox of Sexual Intimacy

DAY 6

"May he grant your heart's desires and make all your plans succeed" (Psalm 20:4 NLT).

As we got to know Regina and Brad as a couple, we learned that whenever Regina thinks of intimacy with Brad, she thinks of extended foreplay. While Brad's thoughts gravitate toward the two of them sharing time together, such as he and Regina holding hands while taking a walk with no specific goal or purpose in mind other than just being together.

After sharing 32 years of marriage together, Regina feels as if their sex life died a few years ago. She often desires sex, but it never seems as if the timing is right. Brad appears tired, doesn't seem interested or it is a late night and one or both of them need to get up early the next morning.

Regina views their sex life as wanting and in need of a much needed boost. Brad on the other hand would rate their sex life as an 8 out of a possible 10, with 10 being ecstatically blissful. He views Regina as sexually responsive yet taking the lead at times—which he likes—and openly sharing her desires and level of satisfaction. When Brad desires sex and makes advances toward Regina, she finds herself having a lot to work through, which often prevents her from responding or initiating the way that she would like to.

> Consider taking the time to pray about your sex life together.

The paradox is that she wants more sexual intimacy but by stuffing her desires repeatedly and keeping her thoughts and emotions to herself, she ends up dismissing Brad's advances. This happens in part because Regina feels it is easier for her to keep silent rather than to talk things out, get her hopes up and find herself once again dealing with disappointment. She surmises what pleasure is there in her having to ask for what she needs because Brad already knows how she feels. But does he?

Talking to each other openly about sexual needs, desires and what pleases them could quite easily take Regina and Brad to the next level of understanding and enjoyment. Sexual intimacy can be a sensitive issue for couples to discuss. It is really important that a safe and comfortable environment be created to have the conversation. To decrease the difficulty in starting the conversation, consult one of the many good Christian books written on the subject. Ask your pastor or counselor for a book recommendation.

Effective questions to ask each other could include topics such as frequency, physical responsiveness, what activity is desired more, what could be omitted or added, etc. Another approach could be to ask each other to rate their sex life using a scale of 1 to 10 and then share what would increase the rating toward a 10.

Scheduling a time to dialogue with your spouse about intimacy is helpful. When it's time for your discussion, light candles, clear the clutter from your bedroom, put on comfortable clothing, sit across from each other and look face-to-face into each other's eyes. Create a mood and a safe non-threatening environment. Most importantly, consider taking the time to pray about your sex life together. Our heavenly Father wants to hear from us about every area of life. Since He created this one, He can also share a creative solution for you.

Remember, the purpose is to connect, not to fight or threaten or blame. Even if you've

REFLECTION
Rate your sex life on a scale of 1 to 10 and see how it compares to your spouse's rating.

rarely ever discussed your intimate relationship or if previous discussions have been on the negative side, you may be pleasantly surprised to learn more about what your spouse desires and what makes him/her feel good. Dialog leads to understanding and deeper connectedness.

DAY 7

Physical Intimacy Starts in Morning

"So be happy with your wife and find your joy with the woman you married— pretty and graceful as a deer. Let her charms keep you happy; let her surround you with her love" (Proverbs 5:18-19 GNT).

Men and women approach sexual intimacy in different ways. The husband's emphasis is often on the physical aspects—the seeing, touching, and climax can become the focus of his attention. The wife, though, comes to sexual intimacy with more interest in the relationship itself. For her, to feel loved, to feel appreciated in word and deed, and to be treated tenderly brings great joy.

Women generally find that emotional connection and being valued leads to sexual desire. Men generally feel sexual desire as a means to feel emotionally connected.

Cultivating deeper sexual intimacy requires understanding and responding to these differences.

The woman's body typically takes longer to arouse and requires emotions to be stirred more than a man's. Intimacy starts long before entering the bedroom or place of love-making. It is established through touch, communication, and loving service. In truth, men don't just want sexual release. They want to be wanted, desired and have an intimate emotional connection as much as women do…only it's met in the process of physical intimacy rather than preceding it.

One of the major areas often ignored in the whole process is the brain—the largest and, we must say, the most ignored sex organ. This is the most misunderstood part of intimacy and sex. Laura Berman, PhD, writes, "The brain is the center for thoughts and emotions, but it is also home to a complex system of nerves, hormones and other chemicals that can affect sexual desire."

> Men and women approach sexual intimacy in different ways.

Your brain is the pleasure center for your body, especially when you have a sexual release.[1]

The significance we give to sex, the attitude we have toward our spouse, the feelings we have about our marriage, are all things that contribute or hinder good feelings and experiences with sex. That thought requires us to ask ourselves, what are we giving each other to think about and what thoughts are we prompting within our spouse throughout the day?

Prompting a desire to have physical intimacy begins when both mates wake up in the morning with a loving greeting for one other. They notice when their partner looks nice and tell them. They treat each other with respect. When they are together, there is physical contact, such as kisses, hugs, a pat on the back, holding hands and touch. They intentionally do nice things for each other such as serve a cup of coffee, put gas in the car, sent a text message, leave a love note in an unexpected location and similar acts of kindness. Occasionally in the morning when we are dressing, brushing our teeth, or doing some other activity and one of us snuggles or fondles the other person, we smile and affectionately say "foreplay begins in the morning." This undoubtedly prompts both of us to smile!

Couples who want to ignite or stoke their romantic flame share the workload. They make time to talk and share thoughts, which for the woman, helps her to feel connected to her husband, and more likely to be "in the mood." As husbands learn to become better listeners, and women open up and share their hearts with their husbands, this helps in creating an atmosphere for deeper intimacy, which leads to shared sexual desire and fulfillment.

As a husband and wife give themselves to each other sexually, they are building a psychological and spiritual bond that unites their souls at the deepest possible level. Together they can face the challenges of life because they are soul partners. Nothing unites a husband and wife more deeply than their sexual bond.

A great sex life grows when both spouses discipline themselves to give to and serve each other. Gary Chapman writes in *Love Is More Than A Feeling*, "God's greatest blessings are offered and received freely. When you freely give yourself to your spouse, and freely receive your spouse to yourself, you nurture your marriage. Sexual intercourse within marriage is designed to give us a taste of the divine and involves the total person."[2]

We've deepened our sexual giving, receiving and satisfaction with each other by sharing from time-to-time about how our bodies have changed, which they will continue to do! Our conversations have included providing practical specific information such as, what once was possible...no longer is, what once felt pleasurable... no longer does, what was not needed before... is needed now.

REFLECTION
Describe why intimacy starts long before entering the bedroom.

CHAPTER 4

Differences that Complement

Wallace and Linda Mitchell

Family Culture

"I press on toward the goal for the prize of the upward call of God in Christ Jesus. Let those of us who are mature think this way, and if in anything you think otherwise, God will reveal that also to you" (Philippians 3:14–15 ESV).

Every family has a distinct way of operating and handling family relationships. As we grow up, we learn to operate within our family culture. When we marry, we each bring our two distinct family cultures with us.

> The reality is that most cultural differences are not right or wrong.

Growing up, most of us have noticed attributes about our family and parents that we didn't like. In light of these experiences, we usually decide that we will not do what our parents did. Consequently we attempt to change what we perceive as negative family patterns. When we change from the things in our family culture that we consider wrong, we believe we have discovered not only a better way but the "best way."

Often unknowingly, we marry a person who has done the same thing with his or her family culture. Now there are two individuals who believe they are right in the changes and adjustments made to improve the state of affairs in their lives and marriage.

Two "right" people who have a disagreement do not easily solve differences. Each one has a tendency to think, "I've already changed the things I needed to change."

When our spouse has a different opinion than our opinion, we often make a judgment. We come to the conclusion that what our spouse thinks is illogical, mistaken, wrong, stubborn, mean, hurtful, insensitive, and the list goes on.

Family Christmas celebrations are examples that demonstrate the multitude of unique cultural differences marriages may experience. Two people, both with fond memories of childhood Christmases, can easily have tensions that escalate into life-sized problems during this season. One spouse remembers how relatives, dressed in their best attire, visited on Christmas Eve. After a big dinner, everyone gathered around the Christmas tree to sing carols, open presents and visit late into the night. The other spouse remembers waking up early Christmas day—the excitement of ripping open presents, lounging around all morning in pajamas and playing with new toys.

When two people are married, they need to decide: "When do we open our presents?" "When do we get together with relatives?"

It's easy to advise, "Oh, they just need to compromise, it's no big deal."

But most solutions are not that simple. The truth is both husband and wife has fond childhood memories printed indelibly in their minds. Problems escalate when one spouse insists the other must celebrate Christmas "their" way rather than the way their spouse remembers. Forcing a spouse to break Christmas traditions or any traditions, for that matter, can lead to severe family tensions. The relationship may survive the first Christmas, but once again the next year, the couple faces the same differences. The possibility of rehashing their opinions and becoming even more irritated with each other increases.

Different ways of celebrating Christmas is one example of many possible cultural differences. The issue is that tensions increase from

REFLECTION
What is or has been your most difficult cultural difference?

hundreds of dissimilarities—money management, sharing household work, activities with friends, raising children and much more. We can disagree about how to hang up our clothes, stack food in the pantry, mow the lawn and in how we will discipline our children.

Personality: Opposites Attract

DAY 2

"So God created man in his own image, in the image of God he created him; male and female he created them" (Genesis 1:27 ESV).

Why do opposites attract? Why on earth does God create us with such different personalities, which results in making it difficult to see eye-to-eye in marriage?

Perhaps we can better understand our differences when we look at Jesus' personality. Because He is perfect, Jesus is the composite of the best personality traits possible. Humans are not perfect, but a husband and wife who complement each other's personality traits more fully reflect the image of God. This is why opposites are often attracted to each other, but not always. Some spouses do share the same personality traits, but this does not mean their relationships are trouble free.

Many spouses find it beneficial to identify each person's personality or behavior style, or have a detailed understanding of the differences. Spouses need to be aware that each personality type has God-given personality traits.

> Learn to complement one another and reflect the fullness of God as a couple.

The DISC Personality Test[1] focuses on four main categories of people's behavioral styles: D (dominance) is the driver, doer, task-oriented person; I (influence) is a people-oriented individual who usually doesn't focus on the task. They like to talk and be around people; S (steadiness) is a person who likes security and small groups. They are sensitive to how people operate, and make a good diplomat; C (conscientiousness) behavioral styles are the detail people. They ask "why" and are good accountants, making sure every "i" is dotted and "t" is crossed. Normally these four behavioral styles intermix and differences can become much more complicated and accentuated. No one has a pure, one-dimension behavioral style.

Here's an example: Emily is energized by people relationships. She isn't as focused on the particular task as long as she has people to talk to. Emily marries Ryan, a detailed guy who likes everything in order and in its place. She looks at her life that is often a bit chaotic, and she finds herself drawn to Ryan because he is so exact and neat. He, in his orderly and perfectionist manner, observes this lively girl as full of life and fun. Since he is often bored with his orderly ways, he thinks, "What a refreshing person." Both are attracted to each other's unique behavioral styles and differences prior to marriage.

Soon after they say "I do," Emily walks into the house, flings her coat haphazardly across the couch and drops her shoes in the hallway, causing Ryan's blood pressure to rise steadily! From his perspective, a coat is not to be thrown across a couch or shoes dropped randomly. The disorder bothers Ryan. He sees nothing but the coat and the shoes lying in disarray. "The place is a mess," Ryan states with obvious frustration. "Please hang up your coat and pick up your shoes!"

Emily responds casually, "Pardon me? What mess? What are you talking about? I'll get around to picking up later, let's just talk a few minutes." Eventually she does pick up her coat and shoes, but in her own time, which is never soon enough for Ryan.

Later in the year, the couple decides to take a vacation. Emily says, "You know what I would love to do? Let's drive to Florida. Let's just take some money and see where the road leads us."

Again, Ryan's heart starts to race, "No plan? No, no, we must have a plan. Give me a map and a highlighter and I will trace a route to Florida, noting the best rest stops, gas stations, places to eat, and Starbucks along the way. I will calculate exactly how much money we will need to go there and back."

Emily's eyes widen in surprise and disappointment. "That's not a vacation! That's a death march! That's no fun. Go by yourself!"

Emily and Ryan's interaction demonstrates the vast differences in personality couples often face. These differences are initiated early in development. When we come into

REFLECTION
What have you learned about your personality through your spouse?

this world, we come with a unique, God-given personality. Granted, as we grow, mature and experience the environment around us, we develop our distinct personality.

Relational Messages

"A woman from Samaria came to draw water. Jesus said to her, 'Give me a drink'" (John 4:7 ESV).

Frequently, a woman projects two messages when she speaks. She's not necessarily doing this on purpose. It is part of her makeup because she tends to be more relational, more aware of the feelings of others and more nurturing than a man.

Most men, on the other hand, are usually driven by goals and the facts. They need a goal, a clear sense of purpose to function, and once they accomplish that goal, they need another one. The facts will keep them on track with the goals.

An example of this would be when a wife asks her husband to do some chores around the house. She requests, "Would you fix the dripping faucet for me?" The husband gives a loosely detailed explanation about why he can't fix it right this moment—he has five other projects that need his immediate attention first. After they are accomplished, he will get to her request. Immediately he recognizes that his wife is not happy.

> Jesus fulfilled His goals but never neglected the building of personal relationships.

If he could rewind the conversation, he may realize that he forgot to look at the relational part of that request. She had asked him to fix something. His response, in her reasoning, rated her at number six of importance in her husband's life. He had five other priorities that were more important than her request.

Probably not thinking this overtly; it's more built into her internal processing, being perceptive and relational. If a husband succeeds in explaining thoroughly the importance of all of his other tasks, he convinces her she is number six on his list, and she will feel like number six. Consequently, a husband can stay in trouble—his logic is good, but he is not answering the relational questions his wife is asking: Do you love me enough to take care of me?

Husbands, if you are wondering what the correct answer to the faucet-fixing question is, try this: "I love you more than anything in the world, and I want to fix the faucet because you are special to me, but I have a couple of things to get finished today. Would tomorrow be okay?" This response answers the wife's relational question and allows the discussion to proceed on a factual level.

When a husband or a wife infers the other is wrong, they are not attempting to understand where the other spouse is coming from. They are thinking in terms of who is right and who is wrong. However, if both the husband and wife see their responses as simply different, they might attempt to understand what is going on within their spouse and endeavor to make appropriate adjustments.

"Understanding that differences are not intentional can make a huge difference in a relationship," states psychologist Michael G. Conner. "The differences that can be sensed between a man and woman can deepen their relationship. More importantly, when men seek to understand and appreciate that which is feminine, they come to a deeper understanding of their self. And when a woman seeks to understand that which is masculine in men, they come to appreciate and understand more about their self."[1]

When husbands and wives learn to accept their differences and make adjustments, they avoid perceiving their differences as personal attempts to frustrate each other.[2] In other words, a husband does not have to become more sensitive and relational like a woman; instead, he can approach the situation so that he allows her to be who God created her to be—sensitive and relational. In this way, he is seeking to understand those underlying relational questions his wife is asking and answer her questions based on their love relationship.

If he embraces her sensitive nature, she will be responsive to those things around her, including her husband. But when a husband keeps ignoring the relational and perceptive aspect of his wife, she may turn off her compassionate and relational part, and experience difficulty remaining sensitive to her husband.

REFLECTION

Does understanding that differences are not intentional improve your relationship with your spouse?

Likewise, wives can be their sensitive, relational selves and still communicate the facts husbands desire in conversation. She needs to attempt to articulate in a way that gives him an avenue to understand her heart. Sometimes a statement like, "I need you to listen to me, but I don't need you to fix anything," can alert the husband to tune in relationally.

Made to Complement

"And the word of the Lord came to me, saying, 'Jeremiah, what do you see?' And I said, 'I see an almond branch.' Then the Lord said to me, 'You have seen well, for I am watching over my word to perform it'" (Jeremiah 1:11–12 ESV).

One day, I desired to communicate an "I love you" message to my wife by cleaning up our kitchen. After I had spent thirty minutes putting things in order, Linda walked by the kitchen door, threw a quick glance into the room and casually said, "Would you pick up the teaspoon and put it in the sink where it belongs?"

> A husband and wife each have unique vision that complements the other. Godly insight comes by sharing and hearing one another.

Now, I had just finished cleaning the whole kitchen, or so I thought. Her casual comment really upset me. *How could she, in one milli-second, see the one thing I didn't do?* Nevertheless, I bit my tongue and picked up the one thing that I had missed, a teaspoon.

Still irritated, I walked down to my basement study and tried to figure out how on earth Linda could in a one milli-second glance see the one thing I didn't do?

I soon went back upstairs and walked into the kitchen where Linda was sitting at the table drinking a cup of tea by the window. Without premeditation I said, "I'd like you to do something for me."

"Sure, what?" she asked. She had no idea that I had been fuming so I casually said, "I want you to glance out the window and then look back at me." She did. I know now that it was God who caused me to ask her, "What did you just see out there?" She quickly answered, "Well, I saw our dogwood tree. The sun is shining down on the tree, and where the sun is hitting, the leaves look kind of yellow, but where it's shaded, it shows a real dark green color. The blossoms are coming out and each has four petals, and they're a beautiful pink with a dark pink edge. The centers are greenish-yellow with stamens sticking out of them. The car is parked out front, and it needs to be washed."

Not only was I stunned by the detail, but also by her instantaneous comprehension of all that information. Again, I realized how different Linda was from me in her basic make-up.

Just then, our fifteen-year-old son walked into the kitchen.

"Son," I said, "I want you to look out the window."

"Why?" he asked.

"Just look out the window," I ordered sternly. "Take a long look."

After a long look, I told him to turn around and tell me what he saw.

"A tree," he said.

"Yes," I agreed, "but can you tell me anything else?"

"It's just a tree, Dad. Nothing but a tree out there!" he grumbled.

"There's more out there than a tree," I countered. "What else?"

He said, "Grass! There's grass!"

Suddenly another light bulb went off in my head. I realized that I walk around in this world and, like my son, see trees and some grass. Linda sees the intricate detail of a tree. She sees individual leaves, petals and also the colors and hues represented.

I realized right then and there another huge difference between the two of us. This time it was not a gender difference—it was a difference in our basic human make-up.

That difference noted, it could also be true that men have this same ability. I remember reading that Ted Williams, a baseball player and one of the greatest hitters of all time, could watch the rotation of the stitching on the ball as it sped toward him. Having observed that, he could predict its final position over the plate four out of ten times at bat.[1] Now that is seeing the details!

Linda is like that. She is extremely observant and sees the details. When I

REFLECTION
Do you and your spouse each have unique vision that complements the other?

recognized her unique talent, I realized that her ability to see the details should not be an irritation but a resource to me. Since I shared that with her, Linda realizes her unique quality and is motivated to share her insights with me. She enjoys sharing and I enjoy listening.

Short Accounts

"Therefore, confess your sins to one another and pray for one another, that you may be healed" (James 5:16 ESV).

It is futile to attempt to change your spouse's family culture or personality or gender specifics. By trying to do so, husbands and wives are in effect destroying the other person, essentially telling them who is wrong.

When you tell someone they are wrong, you generally send them one of three messages: "There is something about you I don't like!" "I don't like you!" Or "I don't love you!"

> A straw can break the camel's back. Keep short accounts.

In marriage, the "you are wrong" messages are similar to little, tiny pieces of straw that pile up over the years to become an enormous pile. One piece of straw after another piled on top of a camel until the last straw added to the pile causes the camel to collapse. At the camel's collapse, couples often (desperately) go to marriage counseling. They attempt to pull out different straws and try to decide which one broke their marriage. We can assure you, it wasn't just one straw—it was the accumulation of the large pile!

Conversely, the "I love you" messages tend to pile on in a very different way. I love you enough to take you out to dinner. I love you enough to fix the faucet. I want to protect your sensitivity. All these constant and reassuring messages that say, "I love you," pile on over the years, and before realizing it, you have grown a dynamic marriage!

When couples come to us for marriage counseling, they usually have a dire issue they are trying to come to grips with. They believe that a certain situation is destroying their marriage. Often that situation is evidence of a history of "I don't love you" messages that have culminated to cause their current state of affairs. The couple may be working on fixing the problem, but they do not often succeed because the situation resulted from years of many accumulated, "piled on" issues.

To begin to bring resolve to a marriage, we suggest that you start pulling out the straws, one at a time. We begin by helping the couple to identify and remove the straws that say, "I don't love you," and replace them with those that speak the message, "I love you!"

Linda and I have a very painful life experience in this area. Our early marriage was filled with "I don't love you" messages. After ten years of these messages, Linda finally shut down emotionally toward me. Somewhere along the way that final straw of, "I don't love you" was piled on. Because I did not realize the messages that I was sending, I did not understand her behavior. Therefore, I reacted with an attitude of, "What's wrong with you?"

For years Linda would express, "You are chipping away at my heart." As we write this now, it sends chills down my spine, but at the time, I could not comprehend what she was talking about. Now I understand exactly what I did to her: I was not hearing her relational heart messages to me. I had ignored them for years.

The night that the final straw broke the camel's back and all she could utter in pain-filled words was, "I'm sorry. I'm sorry, but I don't love you anymore." As a sensitive and relational female, she was sorry for how she felt, but she could not get out from under all the straws that I had piled on and that weighed her down to the breaking point.

Please consider a word of advice from us: Deal with problems when they come up. If you don't, future troubles are built on the issues left unsettled. After a while, husbands and wives will have disagreements built on the cumulative effect of all the other disagreements they've had over all the years, and will find it almost impossible to resolve anything. That possibility should scare every married couple into finding solutions as quickly as possible.

REFLECTION

What does it mean to keep short accounts?

What can you do? You must uncover those issues, deal with them and find forgiveness before you can work with a clean slate and handle conflicts individually as they arise.

Truely Listening

"And he said to him, 'Teacher, all these I have kept from my youth' And Jesus, looking at him, loved him" (Mark 10:20–21 ESV).

The differences between a man and woman are complex and varied. Linda and I are still learning and do not pretend to have all the answers. We do know that with healthy communication, a couple will gain a deeper understanding and appreciation for each other.

Communication is a key. Ultimately, this helps to build the marriage God always intended. When a couple does not understand personality differences, a spouse's responses can cause tremendous pain. Greater understanding of why our spouse reacts the way she or he does helps us see the logic behind their actions.

I realized that some wives like chocolates and others, flowers. Linda preferred that I pick up my clothes and not make a mess in our home. I quickly learned how to give that kind of "I love you" message. We made the choice to endeavor in making a heart connection rather than arguing over a head connection.

Being observant of emotions helps us to make that heart connection. Emotions often communicate what is going on internally and can be red flag warnings to sit up and pay extra close attention to what's really happening.

One morning I left for work. All seemed well between Linda and me. I called her once or twice during the day and we had a pleasant conversation. That evening, I returned home and casually asked, "How are you doing?"

She said, "Fine." The single word answer without any additional comments made me suspicious.

"Are you sure?" I asked. Again, she responded, "Fine."

I was fairly certain that she was not fine. In an effort to be sensitive and understand, I said, "I feel as if something is bothering you and I want to be a part of what you are feeling. Would you let me?"

> One has to truly love to truly listen.

"I don't feel like you are taking care of me," she responded.

Wait a minute. Everything had seemed all right this morning, how could things have gone awry during the eight hours I was not even present?

I said, "Tell me more. How am I not taking care of you? Give me something to grasp."

"You didn't empty the trash. You didn't sweep off the porch," she said.

"Oh, you're right. I will do them right away," I said.

"No, it's all right. Don't bother," she said.

I knew this was something I definitely needed to do. So while I swept the porch, I reasoned, "Why does having a clean or dirty porch have anything to do with not taking care of her?"

The answer became clear. When Linda asked me to empty the trash and sweep the porch and I didn't do them, the message I communicated to her was that I was not taking care of her. Let me restate that. It caused her to feel as if I was not taking care of her. I may be splitting hairs, but this message is a little different from the "I don't love you" message. However, it does help to know exactly what a person is feeling and why they feel the way they do.

Since the unemptied trash has that heart connection, I need to empty the trash. For us, emptying the trash is relational. It communicates that I am taking care of her.

Linda recognized her challenge to articulate her feelings with specific words. She also learned to recognize the fallacy of believing that "Wallace ought to know what to do. If I have to tell him, then it is not worth it." The truth is, Wallace does not know! A wife must articulate what she feels so her husband can understand those inward emotions.

REFLECTION

Should a wife articulate what she feels so her husband can understand her inward emotions?

I learned to be more aware of her thoughts so that I could more easily receive her expressed emotion. When Linda attempts to articulate what she is feeling or perceiving, I can hear her heart and make an effort to understand. Bottom line: She is communicating something I don't always see or understand, but in so doing, we make a more healthy connection.

Pencil, Flower Analogy

"Likewise, husbands, live with your wives in an understanding way, showing honor to the woman as the weaker vessel, since they are heirs with you of the grace of life, so that your prayers may not be hindered" (1 Peter 3:7 ESV).

When we understand how we are made, we can approach conflict with understanding and wisdom. A man needs to realize that having a discussion with his wife is not the same as discussing something with another guy. To illustrate, let's say we have two objects—a pencil and a flower. If a pencil (representing a man) and a flower (representing a woman) is pressed down firmly onto a flat surface repeatedly and under the exact same amount of pressure, the pencil remains unscathed and rigid, but the flower bends, its petals crumple and eventually fall off. This is a picture of what can happen when a husband and wife come into conflict. They have had a disagreement with equal intensity on both sides. The wife can be emotionally damaged by the discussion or conflict, but the husband doesn't think it's a big deal. As a result, many husbands walk away feeling as though they won the battle but ultimately lose the war.

> Facts can win the battle, but just facts will not help us to win the war.

In marriage counseling, when we ask a husband to be aware of the "flower," we are asking him to make a minor adjustment to his thinking. We are not asking him to be less of a man.

We do not ask the wife to be less sensitive and less relational because that would be asking her to stop being *female*! Surely the man doesn't want his wife to stop being female; therefore, we suggest to the man to adjust his thinking. He can do that without becoming damaged and still be masculine.

At the same time, a wife has a responsibility to understand her husband. She needs to remember that he needs facts and goals and is often confused by or misses the relational message. She needs to attempt to articulate her feelings in a way that he understands.

Sometimes Linda will say, "I need to talk to you but I don't need you to fix it!" I breathe a sigh of relief. I know the only goal I have is to listen. Therefore, by listening intently, this problem often will go away after we talk with no other action needed on my part.

A case illustrating these points happened when a lady came for marriage counseling several years ago.

"What seems to be the problem?" I asked. She replied, "I'm crazy!"

"So you really think you're crazy?" I asked.

"Oh yes, I'm crazy," she repeated. "I have a wonderful husband, he has a wonderful job, we have a beautiful home, two new cars, three lovely children, and I'm not happy. So I must be crazy."

I asked what her husband thought. She said that she had talked to her husband many times about her unhappiness but was unable to explain why she felt the way she did. He thought she was unreasonable and that nothing would make her happy. He, being a man, had focused on the task and the facts. He worked harder; he put in more hours at the office and bought her more things, hoping to make her happy.

As we counseled both of them, it became clear that she did not care so much about the house or the cars; she just wanted a close relationship with her husband. In trying to fix the problem, he worked harder and longer to provide "things" to make her happy. By putting more time into his job, he was doing the very thing that took away from what she longed for: his time!

The more he worked, the more she was feeling empty and alone. Through counseling, the couple successfully reached the core of the problem. He was

REFLECTION

Who is the spouse in your family who needs facts and goals and often misses the relational message?

able to make adjustments in his thinking and his lifestyle so he could spend more quality time with his wife. He was beginning to understand her relational needs and messages. She began to feel closer to him because they started to communicate and understand each other more.

CHAPTER 5

For the Love of Money!

Steve and Mary Prokopchak

Disagreement We Struggled to Get Through

Our disagreement started with the weekly grocery bill. Mary and I had previously agreed upon a specific grocery allowance but repeatedly Mary found "deals" that were to somehow "save us money in the future."

In reality, we rarely saw the savings. Our dissension did not involve a large amount of money, but we had three small children while we lived in a very crammed two-bedroom apartment. Every dollar counted and every dollar spent was questioned and accounted for, unfortunately by me (Steve).

To my embarrassment today, I perused each grocery receipt with a fine tooth comb while commenting, "Did we really need this?" or "What does this item have to do with groceries?"

> Every dollar counted and every dollar spent was questioned and accounted for, unfortunately by me.

Mary felt judged and criticized by me and rightly so. I assumed Mary didn't care about the budget or how hard I worked for those grocery dollars. She found my assessment upsetting. The spirit of our weekly conversations was negative, defeating and harmful to our financial and emotional health.

Initially we negatively labeled Mary a "spender" and Steve as "tight." If we had stopped with that terminology, our differences would have escalated over time and become even more hurtful. We did not intend to have ill will toward one another. We both desired to stay within our budget and provide for our family, but we pursued the goal differently. Eventually our struggle to resolve our disputes revealed that we actually had different financial values.

Mary's gift was being a "giver" and Steve's was an "investor." That means that part of Mary's love language is to give to others. Part of Steve's is to save for the future. Neither is wrong, just different. Until we discovered how to value each other's perspective and to incorporate both into our cooperative efforts, we had an ongoing difference. Proverbs 20:3 wisdom is to avoid strife and not to be quick to quarrel.

REFLECTION

How can differing financial views become a cooperative strength to your marriage relationship?

That verse is tough to apply whenever we have differing values, which are deeply rooted in our belief system. Values do not change easily; and we are more vigilant to maintain and hold tightly onto them rather than compromise.

Mary and I learned to merge our two conflicting financial values to create a better, cooperative value. Today, we have discovered a financial strength in our marriage by incorporating both of the differing values. Mary brings what Steve does not and vice versa. Together our values merge with a better picture of the whole. Today we are both saving more and giving more than ever. We have discovered the blessing of both perspectives and have acclimated to what was previously deep opposition.

Debt Is Killing Us

Are you aware that the average American family has a consumer debt of $16,140? The average mortgage debt is $155,361 and the average student loan debt is $31,946 and climbing. The total debt American consumers owe is $11.85 trillion as of 2015, according to an online article written by Tim Chen titled *American Household Credit Card Debt Statistics: 2015.*[1]

How much are we saving? The average savings account balance in the U.S. was $5,923 in 2011. How long could you live on a total savings of $6,000 while maintaining credit card debt, car loan debt, college loans and mortgages? No wonder couples struggle with disagreements about money issues in marriage more than any other area. Most couples know how to charge, but taking responsibility and agreeing on how to pay for debt can be a disturbing process.

From the website Debt.org, bankruptcy filings came to an all-time high in 2005 with more than two million initiated.[2] That was one in every 55 households. Today, consumers file for more bankruptcies than businesses do.

Due to Mary's and my personal merged financial values, we really dislike indebtedness unless it is for the purchase of an asset. Far too many couples live from paycheck to paycheck. They purchase liabilities and go into debt for them. Liabilities are purchases that actually lose value once purchased (cars, clothes, furnishings and adult toys such as boats and other recreational items). Assets are purchases that gain value after purchasing (investments such as land, houses, retirement accounts or a small business on the side). As we grow assets, we grow wealth. As we live out of liabilities, we deplete our net worth.

Are you purchasing assets or liabilities?

What is your financial value as a couple? Do you purchase a lot of liabilities or assets? Do you pay off your credit card balance in full each month or do you carry a balance? Proverbs 22:7 offers perspective when it reminds us that the borrower is servant to the lender.

Are you servant to a bank, a credit card company or your parents?

Gaining interest on investments is far better than paying exorbitant interest rates on debt. Mary and I recently checked on the interest rate of our personal credit card's line of credit. I had to catch my breath when I read the 24.99% interest rate!

We are fully convinced that God's heart for His people is to be free of debt connected to a liability. God desires us to grow wealth so that we can sow wealth. The larger our debt, the less we will be able to give to help the needy; the less we will be able to help our children with college and the less we will have set aside for the future when we are no longer able to work.

If God calls you to the mission field, but you carry thousands of dollars in college debt, you will need to delay your obedience to that call and work on the massive pile of educational debt first. Many people have confided that their only asset is their home, which they are working to pay off early. That early pay off part is great and to be encouraged, but at the end of the day, you have to live somewhere. Your home should not be your one and only asset.

A number of years ago we met with a young, newly married couple that had six-figure indebtedness in college loans. The couple filed for a reduction in the monthly payback of the loan. They desired to make payments that were lower than the actual interest charges on the loans. We posed this question, "Do you realize that in ten or twenty years you will actually owe more money

REFLECTION
Do you have a plan to pay off consumer debt?

on your school loans than you owe today?" They had no realization of this certainty.

Place to Start: It's All God's

The book of Proverbs is packed full of financial wisdom for marriages. Solomon was the wealthiest man of his time and had exceptional wisdom to go along with his financial prowess.

In our Bibles, Mary and I have highlighted each verse that connects the use of money or a financial principle. Subsequently, we attempt to incorporate those principles into our lives and beliefs. We have endeavored to appropriately place highly valuable scriptures alongside the financial principles we have learned.

Although there are no guarantees to prosperity, biblical principles of wisdom can help us avoid disasters.

Generosity is a sign of maturity in the believer's life.

The place to start is the topic of generosity. Although generosity should be from the heart, at first, giving is more like a test of ownership. As one gives and continually discovers a return in multiple ways, giving becomes a lifestyle. Generosity is a sign of maturity in the believer's life. Generosity is also subjective. Jesus noticed the generosity of the widow placing a mite in the collections. Jesus seems to base generosity more upon what we have left than what we give (See Mark 12:43, 44). Through everything we do, we need to incorporate a spirit of generosity; it is life to others and to our marriages. "Give and it will be given unto you" (Luke 6:30). Proverbs 24:9 articulates, "A generous man will himself be blessed, for he shares his food with the poor."

Next is the honest confession and scriptural truth that states God gives us the power and the opportunity to create and possess wealth. This confession is where it begins for us. The scripture reveals, "He did all this so you would never say to yourself, 'I have achieved this wealth with my own strength and energy. Remember the Lord your God. He is the one who gives you power to be successful, in order to fulfill the covenant He confirmed to your ancestors with an oath'" (Deuteronomy 8:17, 18).

If God provides and shares wealth with us, our accumulation is all His. We are only stewards of that which He shares with us. When we tithe (give a tenth of our income), the remaining 90 percent is not ours. One hundred percent is His. Ten percent to our local church as a tithe is a starting point, our first step of obedience in honoring the One who provides it all. We sow offerings and firstfruits to others in missions and in select spiritual projects in order to help change lives. "Honor the Lord with your wealth, with the firstfruits of all your crops; then your barns will be filled to overflowing, and your vats will brim over with new wine" (Proverbs 3:9, 10).

This is the first step in our own financial discipline. It is a step that says Jesus is Lord of our

REFLECTION

Do we pray about our giving and generosity?

finances. It is caring for the poor and the marginalized. It is saying that our wealth is not simply ours alone, but God's and He can use it for His purposes. "A generous man will prosper; he who refreshes others will himself be refreshed" (Proverbs 11:25).

Creative Budgeting Ideas

Although a piece of paper with figures on it will not keep anyone from spending, it will reveal where your money is going. Creating a budget is a picture of income and expenses. If you put on paper exactly what is coming in and what is going out, you'll obtain a helpful snapshot.

A budget, if used correctly, can help maintain discipline and provide a picture of where your finances are designated. A budget should reflect a whole year and not a mere month, due to the fact there are numerous annual and semi-annual expenses. Remember to be as generous as possible with your family's needs because, "A greedy man brings trouble to his family" (Proverbs 15:27).

Remaining accountable with our finances and our budgets should be a key goal. I (Steve) am first accountable to God and then to my spouse. I am accountable to provide for my family. The proper use of finances calls for a certain level of accountability. The people who view finances as their own to do with whatever they desire will most certainly encounter financial difficulty. Each spouse needs a level of accounting for those monies earned and spent. It

> A budget, if used correctly, can help maintain discipline and provide a picture of where your finances are designated.

may be a parent, a spouse or a financial advisor, but someone more knowledgeable than yourselves should have the freedom to speak into your financial decisions regularly.

Spousal accountability has saved many husbands from disastrous business propositions. Solomon wrote that ill-gotten treasures are of no value (Proverbs 10:2). When we are repeatedly handed something of value for which we did not labor, we will not appreciate its true worth. "Dishonest money dwindles away, but he who gathers money little by little makes it grow" (Proverbs 13:11).

Work at making financial decisions together and ahead of time as much as possible. Many purchases are emotional or spontaneous and not well thought out, especially with the easy availability of credit. A rule of thumb with most purchases is to wait one month. If you still need the item and have the needed finances designated after thirty days, make the purchase. Obviously this takes patience and discipline. Retailers are banking on your emotional response to a sale or to an advertisement. Financial decision-making is all about discipline. We love the principle in Proverbs 24:27, which teaches, "Finish your outdoor work and get your fields ready; after that, build your house."

With this principle in mind, establish two purchase lists: a need list and a wish list. The need list is an agreement to purchase as the funds become available and the wish list is a purchase when we have extra, non-designated funds available. Ask yourselves, "Do we really need this or is it a want?"

Another good question is, "Why do we need this and do we need it right now?" It is amazing how many sale items, together or individually, we can purchase or accumulate and never use or even need them.

Make use of cash as often as possible, especially when in the retail environment (the mall). Studies indicate that we spend 30 percent more money when using a credit card than with cash. Cash leaving our hands provides more thought, more consideration. Although antiquated, writing a check or using a checking debit card is similar.

When using credit cards, use them properly. Credit card companies are in the business of hoping to collect interest off of your purchases. Never give them the opportunity. Pay off every month's balance in full. Whenever you cannot pay the complete balance in any given month or at the most two, stop using the credit card, stop charging. "Just as the rich rule the poor, so the borrower is servant to the lender" (Proverbs 22:7). No matter from whom we borrow, we become their servant.

REFLECTION
How can we be more disciplined purchasers?

DAY 5

Be Your Own Banker

Create a savings account of $2,000 to $3,000 to use as your "credit card" or "consumer loan." When the refrigerator or the car breaks down, borrow from that savings account rather than from another source. When you do borrow from your short-term savings, pay the full amount back so it will be available for future needs. As you pay the loan back to yourself on a monthly basis, you will not have additional interest charges because it is from your own fund. Having a savings account does not mean you are trusting in those riches. Instead you are wise by providing in advance for unexpected expenses. "Whoever trusts in riches will fall, but the righteous will thrive like a green leaf" (Proverbs 11:28).

> Having a savings account does not mean you are trusting in those riches.

Any savings in addition to the emergency fund should go into another account such as a money market account with check-writing privileges. This secondary savings should reach a higher amount to enable you to pay for larger purchases such as updating your vehicle. As this fund grows, it can also provide for you and your family in case of a long-term unemployment period (three to six months).

Were you aware that Proverbs wisely informs us to stay away from being security or surety for another? This means co-signing a loan that requires you to make the payments if the primary party defaults. Unless you have a lot of money at your disposal, you could lose your home from the default process. "Do not be a man who strikes hands in pledge or puts up security for debts; if you lack the means to pay, your very bed will be snatched from under you" (Proverbs 22: 26, 27; see also Proverbs 11:15).

To save in order to purchase assets rather than liabilities will create long-term wealth for you. Many people today live from paycheck to paycheck, and teach their children to do the same. Or, they live from loan to loan. When their children desire to purchase their first car, the parents introduce them to their banker, which can result in a life-long relationship with consumer debt, allowing others to earn money off of their purchases. If you were the one lending, you would be earning the interest. But in order to lend, you must have cash reserves—the asset of a savings account working for you. When you are borrowing, you do not own. When you are the one loaning, you are the one owning.

Be resourceful when spending. Have a contest with your spouse to see which one of you can purchase a needed item at the best price. Barter for babysitting. Trade your items or talents for needed items. For example, you can trade labor by assembling a friend's new furniture in return for his completing your electrical work. Have a yard sale rather than hoarding unused items. Watch for slightly used items at flea markets and on web sites that specialized in advertising second-hand items.

REFLECTION

How can you be resourceful instead of spending money?

Being your own banker will have multiple financial benefits to you as a couple.

Schedule Money Dates

Have you and your spouse ever thought about starting a small business? Many persons have created internet businesses by selling handmade jewelry, yard sale items, estate finds or cars purchased for resale. You can also sell old books or toys online. Stick with what you know and enjoy. It can be a fun and income-producing process. I (Steve) cut and sold firewood to send our children to private school. Later I resold cars on the side to help with college tuition and expenses. "All hard work brings a profit, but mere talk leads to poverty. The wealth of the wise is their crown" (Proverbs 14:23, 24).

> Cooperate as a team and be accountable to each other

Many persons grow their own food in a backyard garden or join a food co-op to save grocery money. Always make wise use of coupons or store specials. Did you know that most food sales repeat themselves weekly or monthly? Ask the person behind the meat counter when your favorite meat will go on sale. Store personnel know the sale schedule.

Schedule regular times with your spouse to review finances and financial goals. Have a weekly or monthly date to discuss income and outgoing expenses to help attain shared financial goals. Cooperate as a team: openly discuss every financial matter, be accountable to each other and determine who of you is better at accounting and able to oversee monthly accounts.

Often one spouse excels at earning and the other at controlling expenses. If you are not good at controlling expenses, humble yourself and delegate the job or at least agree upon a spending limit. For example, perhaps your agreed upon limit is that $25 can be spent on an item without consulting with your spouse. Remember to limit the number of $25 purchases because several purchases quickly accumulate.

When Steve and I agree ahead of time to a plan, we also agree to the sacrifices that will need to be made. This level of agreement and communication can stop the fighting and arguing over finances. Amos 3:3 asks the question of how can two walk together unless they have agreed to do so?

Consequently, when we found agreement in our budgeting practices and our spending, we found a place of power. It was empowering for us to be on the same page financially. We also realized that disagreements had kept us from unity in a crucial part of our marriage.

It can be extremely helpful to record all of your spending for several months—every penny. We did this for one whole year and found that the miscellaneous category in our budget was much larger than indicated. Why? It was the accumulation of those small purchases at minute markets, the supermarkets and discount stores. When we create a thorough record—as painful as it sounds—all of the unknowns become known—nothing is hidden. In the end, we'll have a far more realistic budget the following year.

As you live in moderation, exercise self-discipline, and are generous with others, you will discover more and more leftover money each month. Money and how we make use of it is actually an outside indicator of who we are internally. Listen to these insightful words of Jesus. "Whoever can be trusted with very little can also be trusted with much, and whoever is dishonest with very little will also be dishonest with much. So if you have not been trustworthy in handling worldly wealth, who will trust you with true riches? And if you have not been trustworthy with someone else's property, who will give you property of your own?" (Luke 16:10-12). Our Lord actually indicated that how we handle our money relates to how we handle His spiritual riches.

REFLECTION
Have we considered ways to earn extra cash in order to pay down our debt or meet forthcoming needs?

Plan Annual Evaluation Weekend

DAY 7

Steve and I have found repeatedly that integrity is the glue that holds financial decisions together. God desires to prosper us, but righteousness is His requirement. "Prosperity is the reward of the righteous." How does that happen? Because "the righteous hate what is false." Further, the scripture reveals, "Righteousness guards the man of integrity" (Proverbs 13: 5, 6, 21).

Dishonesty in any way, shape or form will have a direct consequence on finances. We dare not cheat God, the government or our employer and expect to prosper. Sometimes it takes humility to admit that we were wrong and made a mistake, but the Lord honors humility. "Humility and the fear of the Lord bring wealth and honor and life" (Proverbs 22:4).

True wealth is far beyond money, houses and land, silver or gold. Solomon discovered even among all of his possessions something far superior in value. He said, "By wisdom a house is built, and through understanding it is established; through knowledge its rooms are filled with rare and beautiful treasures" (Proverbs 24: 3, 4).

> The security of every child today is not material items, but the unconditional, unwavering and consistent love of parents.

Our home had four bedrooms, three for our two sons and one daughter—truly our "treasures." As a father and a mother, we, personally, could not meet all of our children's needs, but we made sacrifices to be assured that all of their needs were met. (For example: our daughter had a gift to sing and play piano. Due to our lack of knowledge in that area, we hired someone who could meet the need to train her.)

By far, our children's biggest need is for their parents to share the love of God and His desire to be the One who meets all of their needs. The children's second essential need is for their mother and father to love and respect each other. We do not believe there is a child today who is better off with video games and stuff rather than loving, committed parents. No child cares about the math principles taught in school if his/her parents are divorcing. The security of every child today is not material items, but the unconditional, unwavering and consistent love of parents.

For us, that meant taking seriously the need to regularly evaluate our finances. One of the annual ways we did this was to get away for an evaluation weekend, just the two of us.

Have you and your spouse ever considered a personal marriage retreat for the purpose of evaluating the past year and then praying about vision for the forthcoming year? We have been doing this for many years and find it to be one of the most helpful annual connections we share. It gets us on the same page. We take a hard look at what was and evaluate where we are. We keep the excitement factor up by looking ahead toward the future. We review and rewrite, as needed, our marriage mission statement and then write goals for the coming year.

Praying together as a couple is a key to this time.

- Give thanks for God's provision and protection through-out the past year.
- Pray about this time together, specifically that you will hear the voice of your heavenly Father.

- Pray over your marriage, your family, your employment, your finances; pray about everything and anything.

- Give God praise for the positive and the not so positive.

Next, take time to review your budget from the prior year. Where was your budget accurate and where did it miss the mark? Review each of your accounts, checking and savings. Review your giving, including tithe, missions, and offerings. Review your investments such as life insurance, money market, IRA's and so forth. Review your debt and your plan to be clear of debt. Are you in agreement with your saving, life investments and giving? Are you in agreement with any debt you carry? Are you meeting your financial goals in all the above areas?

REFLECTION
What are our most valued treasures?

After evaluation turn toward the future: What are financial goals? What are we saving toward? How are we handling our children's higher education? When do we update our vehicle? What projects do we need to consider in our home to address ongoing maintenance or improvements?

Why do all this? Proverbs 3:9 tells us to honor the Lord with our wealth. We believe He is honored when we are cooperating in financial oneness.

CHAPTER 6

Keeping Your Marriage Vibrant

Duane and Reyna Britton

DAY 1

Roommate or Soul Mate?

When most people hear the word intimacy, they think of sex. But physical sexual intimacy is only an aspect of overall intimacy. Intimacy is having a very close connection with another, which includes every part of the individual—physical, emotional, intellectual and spiritual. Complete intimacy is reserved for husbands and wives.

One complaint from couples we have heard over the years is that their mate doesn't connect with them emotionally. At times their marriage feels as if they are roommates instead of soul mates. Over time it seems as if a wall or swinging door has come between them, short-circuiting their emotional connection.

> Emotional connections are a glue that holds couples together.

The reality is that if a couple doesn't continually nurture their relationship, they will experience a subtle creeping distance between them over time. A marriage lacking intimacy will become functional as if on auto pilot. Emotional connections are a glue that holds couples together. They fertilize the relationship resulting in a joint sense of well-being. Yet it is challenging for many couples to experience such completeness.

Emotions set the mood of the relationship. One of the most important things you can do to restore intimacy to your marriage is to devote attention to each other. Make plans and then follow through with increasing the amount of time that you spend together. These are important contributors to recovering that sense of "us-ness."

Proverbs 21:5 [NLT] says, "The plans of the diligent lead to profit as surely as haste leads to poverty."

It is often said, "Those who plan, plan to succeed, and those who do not plan, plan to fail."

When a couple experiences emotional separation, they should learn how to move on from the past and get to the place where they share the real essence of who they are. It helps to pay attention to and label your own emotions. Many of us have two words to describe our emotions: happy or angry. But dozens of emotions exist between those two words.

We have worked with dozens of married couples over the years that utilized too few words to describe their emotions. We provided them with a printed glossary[1] of emotional expressions and instructed them to have it on hand when they begin talking to each other. The words would provide assistance in helping them further identify, express and clarify what they were feeling.

Emotional intimacy more comfortably occurs after people feel free to express concern and understanding of feelings to each other. Couples benefit from times of sharing and listening to one another, but they also need time together enjoying shared activities such as mutually enjoyable hobbies, antiquing, biking, working out, going to movies, traveling, bird-hunting, hiking, kayaking or going for drives. These shared activities promote pleasurable interactions that evoke positive emotions helping to maintain and increase emotional intimacy.

There are other verbal and non-verbal aspects that enhance the emotional connectivity between couples such as eye contact during conversation, genuine care and regard for each other's best interest, openness about a variety of topics, expressed appreciation and physical touch.

Think about it: Feelings are often our spontaneous, emotional responses to what we encounter through our five senses. If you see a fire truck racing down the road, you may feel troubled or concerned. If your spouse touches your hand,

REFLECTION
Name some verbal and non-verbal aspects that enhance emotional connectivity.

winks at you across the room or blows you a kiss, you feel a loving connection. When we share our emotions with each other and create shared emotions through enjoyable activities, we strengthen our emotional intimacy.

Are We Really Different Emotionally?

DAY 2

"Let us therefore make every effort to do what leads to peace and to mutual edification" (Romans 14:19).

Emotional intimacy occurs when trust and communication between both spouses allow them to share their innermost selves. Deep emotional intimacy is when a person feels wholly accepted, respected and admired in the eyes of their spouse even after they've shared their innermost struggles, fears, failures, successes and proud moments. Many relationships are ruined because of not being sensitive to the emotions of the spouse.

Often researchers conclude that marriages do not fall apart from arguments or even from a lack of sex. Marriages generally begin breaking apart from the lack of emotional intimacy. Over time, a marriage lacking intimacy can become predictable, wanting and lifeless.

Our emotions develop early in our lives. As children grow, they should learn to express their emotions in healthy ways and learn to understand the emotional

> Marriages generally begin breaking apart from the lack of emotional intimacy.

content of other people's verbal and non-verbal communication. Human beings were created to express their emotional needs. To be healthy, everyone needs to be able to explore his emotions and encouraged to express them within a loving relationship.

Four basic emotional needs of everyone include the following:

1. **Affection** Every person needs to know and feel that they are loved. We need to express our love to each other regularly. This can be done by simply saying, "I love you" on a frequent basis. Affection can be expressed to a spouse through intentional caring actions, affection and other non-verbal expressions.

2. **Acceptance** No one likes to be scolded or criticized. Spouses are usually well aware of their own imperfections. By embracing how God unconditionally accepts you, you can then offer the gift of acceptance to your spouse. "Accept one another, then, just as Christ accepted you, in order to bring praise to God" (Romans 15:7 NLT).

3. **Appreciation** Every person desires acknowledgment and appreciation for their achievements, performances, and attained improvements. Demonstrating appreciation may change a couple's attitude toward each other. Appreciation motivates a person to continue with positive actions.

4. **Affirmation** To affirm something is to confirm its truth, worth and strength. To affirm your mate is to honor your mate. Seize the opportunity and privilege to speak a blessing to your spouse by giving your support, approval, encouragement and presence.

In emotional intimacy, couples allow room for growth that leads to a deepening relationship. Emotional intimacy fosters compassion and support, which provides a firm attractive foundation for a marriage to last a lifetime.

REFLECTION

How do you express appreciation to each other?

Emotional awareness requires us to pay attention to feelings, identify them, and think of possible reasons for them. Even if we did not learn how to be emotionally intimate while growing up, we can learn as adults.

Deepening emotional intimacy occurs when both spouses perceive what they are feeling, convey those feelings to each other, and express acceptance and understanding to each other. An often repeated saying reminds us: "Sometimes it's better to be kind than right. We don't need a brilliant mind that speaks, but a patient heart who listens"—anonymous.

Keeping It Real

DAY 3

"But you desire honesty from the womb, teaching me wisdom even there" (Psalm 51:6 NLT).

"Oh my goodness here we go again. You're on my case because I don't want to talk about my day before we go to sleep. It's been a stressful, long day and I am ready to go to sleep."

Upon hearing his response, Keisha turns over to roughly puff up her pillow in demonstration of how frustrated she is that

> Express what you want or need and the feelings you have experienced.

Ryan hardly ever wants to communicate and just spend time connecting with her. She had been waiting until the evening's activities were done, the bedroom TV was off and all was quiet so that she and Ryan could talk and be together. But the same scene had repeated itself again, no conversation, not even a listening ear. Before long, Ryan was asleep and Keisha was sulking while she read Facebook posts.

Just about every marriage has topics or issues that are difficult to discuss. Among couples, the issues vary, but not the response. Uncomfortable feelings and changes in body language, and even in attitudes, flicker as soon as the unpleasant topic is mentioned. Consequently, it is difficult to proceed with meaningful discussion.

Whenever dissentious topics arise, one spouse often feels as if he or she is entering a mine field and tip toes around the subject, fearing an explosion may occur at any moment. Often, it becomes easier to engage in "avoidance" rather than press through into a conversation, because hostility without a predictable outcome could result.

What Keisha really wants from Ryan is connection, an expression of his relationship with her. She does not want to badger him or to feud. She expects Ryan to express or demonstrate his connection with her by engaging in conversation with her. When Keisha is able to move beyond her feelings of rejection, hurt or disappointment and share with Ryan what she really wants, she is in a better place to be clear about how she was feeling when she didn't get it. Her honesty about what she wants from Ryan will help them to explore possibilities on how her need for connection with him can be met.

As a couple working through our own sensitive issues and difficult conversations, we've learned that before one of us starts a difficult conversation, we need to identify for our self what it is that we want or don't want out of the conversation and then share that with the other person.

When starting a sensitive conversation, it is easy for my spouse to think that I am attacking him, especially if my comments are going to be tied to his actions. Often times we want the same things, but obstacles like sensitive feelings or past argumentative conversations get in the way.

For example, my dear husband often miscalculates the number of things he needs to get accomplished and the amount of time it will take to accomplish them before we leave to enjoy some time away. I often feel annoyed at being forced to wait instead of leaving for our trip. I began a conversation to help him understand my frustrations, by saying what I wanted him to understand, how I am feeling and what I am working through. After I shared my annoyances, we both helped each other to understand that we both wanted to have left earlier. Needless to say, we were both in a better frame of mind to tackle things together and were in a better frame of mind when we left.

We make it a goal, that before heading into a touchy conversation, we are intentional to ask ourselves, what is it that we want to accomplish? Is it to be heard, express disappointment, settle on a solution, share how the other person's actions affect me, and so forth? When we identify what we want, we start the conversation expressing our intent. This helps our spouse to focus, feel more at ease and listen to what we are saying, versus wondering where this conversation is going. In a difficult conversation, it is too easy to think or assume that my spouse has an alternate motive or issue.

The next time you need to initiate a difficult conversation with your spouse, pray and ask the Lord to help you to clarify what you are feeling and to identify what it is that

you really want or need. Then create a safe, non-threatening atmosphere. Express what you want or need and the feelings you have experienced. Trust the Lord to bring resolution and to strengthen your relationship with your spouse.

Intellectual Intimacy

DAY 4

"A wise man is strong. A man of much learning adds to his strength" (Proverbs 24:5 NLV).

A small child came home from Sunday school and told his mother: "The teacher told us how God made the first man and the first woman. He made man first, but the man was very lonely with no one to talk to, so God put the man to sleep, and while he was asleep, God took out his brains and made a woman out of them."

If you take a look at popular culture today, you might get the same impression this small child had about men—that men are pretty inept in their roles at home and in top positions of leadership. In many movies and television programs, it's the women who are in positions of authority, leading the team or making critical decisions that turn the situation around.

Do these fairly common portrayals by script writers hinder the intellectual intimacy we are designed to have as couples? It does if one gender thinks the other is intellectually deficient, or another superior. This generalization is not to infer that there are not intelligent women who are capable of leading great organizations and determining solutions that lead to success.

> Intellectual intimacy is best defined as being able to be yourself without fear that your thoughts or ideas will be rejected or demeaned by your spouse.

Not much is taught about the intellectual intimacy we are to experience as couples. Discussing thoughts, theories or philosophies about topics such as food, finances, health, crime, work and even politics, enables spouses to better understand each other. The myth that intellectual intimacy is about discussing highly intellectual ideas (even though this can be fun at times) needs to be expelled.

Psychologist Laura Dawn Davis in her book, *Eight Stages of Intimacy*[1](Couples Company, Inc.), wrote that couples should know whether they have solid intellectual intimacy. She designed a small questionnaire to help them determine their level of intimacy. You and your spouse have solid intellectual intimacy if you can answer "Yes" to all of these situations:

1. **Both you and your partner** know what each of you fear and both make an effort to keep each other from those situations and stimuli.

2. **Opinions, even those you don't agree on, can be stated,** argued and acknowledged without fear of ridicule, abandonment or abuse. (This is especially true for such heated issues as current affairs and politics, about which you may strongly disagree).

3. **Without realizing it**, you and your partner often mirror each other's actions, gestures and speaking style.

4. **You know your partner's life goals**, hopes and dreams.

If your answers are not where you want them to be, begin exchanging ideas. Duane and I have done this by sharing our impressions about current affairs, work and the issues that we think and care about, thoughts about life in general, or specific areas of interests such as places we'd like to travel or some of the things on our "bucket list."

Make sure you do this exchange in a caring, listening and inquisitive context. That means having a willingness to entertain new thoughts and ideas. Caring results in giving each other the mutual freedom to think independently so one partner does not dominate the other or demand that the spouse thinks the same way about everything. Intellectual intimacy is best defined as being

REFLECTION

It is not uncommon for both individuals to believe the other person has more to change than themselves.

able to be yourself without fear that your thoughts or ideas will be rejected or demeaned by your spouse.

If you spend time discussing ideas and dreams, you are well on the way of creating a deeper level of intellectual intimacy within your marriage.

Conquering Challenges Through Devotion

"Go and proclaim in the hearing of Jerusalem this is what the Lord says, remember the devotion of your youth how as a bride you followed me through the wilderness through a land not sown" (Jeremiah 2:2).

Before couples marry, they often view their fiancée idealistically—through the eyes of how and who they want them to be, not how they are. The missing elements, excesses or annoyances are mere coincidental glitches, which they are confident they can help their spouse overcome after they are married. Each one is most likely convinced that he or she will easily conform their spouse to their way of thinking because it's the best way.

It is not uncommon for both individuals to believe the other person has more to change than themselves. Initially these glitches are smothered over by the fresh, whole-hearted devotion, coupled with excited anticipation that newlyweds experience. Jennifer Schuchmann shares in the book, *"What We See In Each Other"* (Couples' Devotional

Bible (NIV), Zondervan, Week of November 4), "The success of a marriage comes, not in finding who we think initially is the 'perfect' person for us, but in our willingness to adjust to the real person we married."

When the marriage begins, both the husband and wife are often a bit "rough around the edges." What we mean by that is they need to learn how to adapt to each other through the struggles and trials they'll face. Challenges faced and endured together forge a strengthening bond. Couples who hold hands, touch and agree together in prayer experience greater melding and merging. "Those who abandon ship, the first time it enters a storm, miss the calm beyond. And the rougher the storms weathered together, the deeper and stronger real love grows" Ruth Bell Graham [EBook *Once A Day Everyday ... For a Woman of Grace* Day 316, Madeline Freeman, Worthy Publishing].

> Why are marriages often decimated when quality time together is lacking?

We are especially saddened whenever we hear that a couple has given up the fight for their marriage after they've weathered several storms and many years together. Why? They are actually forfeiting the best part. They're missing out on the divine dividends derived from earlier years of marital sacrifice, perseverance and devotion—all ingredients that richly mature a marriage over time.

We often ask ourselves why any couple wants to surrender the prize of a marriage that endures, a marriage that evokes ever increasing fruitfulness and love for each other. When couples enjoy the fruit of their committed, enduring devotion to each other, the relationship radiates a visual demonstration to others. It inspires other couples to desire more for their marriage. It creates hope that helps them to persevere through the rough spots and to grow in love for each other, because loves endures.

"Love never gives up, never loses faith, is always hopeful, and endures through every circumstance" (1 Corinthians 13:7 NLT). It is true that devotion and the feeling of love can wane over time. Responsibilities, family, jobs, ever-increasing electronic connectivity, the world at our door steps, even the joyful rewarding aspects of life can slowly erode the love and devotion that couples experience. Marriages are often decimated when quality time together is lacking and love and passion are waning, while facing unexpected or prolonged periods of challenges.

REFLECTION

The Lord, without fail, sends delightful surprises along the way: things that we did not plan or even imagine.

Despite the challenges that life brings, the prophet Jeremiah was instructed by the Lord to declare to His people that these are truly difficult times and a tough place to be, but what will get you through this is to remember…to recall the devotion you had in your earlier years. It will compel you to follow God through the barren places, where the way was rough and the going was difficult with little evidence of fruit. As you pray and persevere together, be confident that seasons of fruitfulness will indeed come.

We consistently find that the Lord, without fail, sends delightful surprises along the way: things that we did not plan or even imagine.

Mutual Plans Strengthen Marriages

"May He grant you your heart's desire and fulfill all your plans" (Psalm 20:4).

We go away each year between Christmas and New Year's Day. This time is spent committing ourselves to the Lord, reviewing the past year, acknowledging the joys that we've experienced, challenges and successes we've encountered and celebrating our love for each other. Each year, without fail, we are filled with gratitude toward God as we recall His goodness and faithfulness.

This results in times of spontaneous prayer together throughout our time away. We also spend time planning the year ahead. The extent of our planning includes our priorities both individually as well as a couple. Our goal planning for the coming year takes into account time to be spent with our adult children/extended family members, our vocation, business and ministry goals and leisure activities.

One recent year we listed our desires to visit our adult children, their families and our extended family members. All of who, with the exception of one daughter and her family, live several states away or on the opposite coast. To travel and spend time with them was a major undertaking in time and expense. It didn't seem quite possible for us to arrange or afford it, but we placed the specifics of the trip along with a potential timeframe on our list of plans for the coming year.

A few months passed. Much to our excitement, a joint window of time and the finances became available for us to purchase the airline tickets and make the associated arrangements. Our plans, enabled by God's favor and provision, became quite the testimony to our family as we shared the details of how our desire of spending quality time with them became a reality.

The Lord's ways are high above ours and beyond our understanding. We don't always see the fulfillment of our annual plans and desires. Sometimes we'll drop them as the year unfolds because the Lord opens new doors of opportunity or other unanticipated things become a priority. Sometimes we list an unfulfilled plan again for the upcoming year.

The end-of-the-year-time away, reviewing the past year and looking forward to the next year along with including our "heart's desires plans," continues to be something that we both excitedly look forward to every year. We make sure that we both talk and listen to each other (without interrupting). These planning times benefit our relationship. It's not just the plan that is important, but connecting together as husband and wife.

Over the years we consistently find that the Lord, without fail, sends delightful surprises along the way: things that we did not plan or even imagine. One such delightful surprise was a completely unanticipated ministry opportunity. Although it required a major change that happened as a "suddenly," we both were blessed by it. Our marriage has been

REFLECTION
How do you plan together for future goals and dreams?

strengthened because the delightful surprise created the means for us to serve out of our sweet spots, both collectively and individually. We feel the continual blessedness of this unfolding truth—"Commit your works to the Lord and your plans will be established" (Proverbs 16:3).

DAY 7

Reciprocal Fun

"Always be joyful" (1 Thessalonians 5:16 NLT).

As a couple, we value the multiple benefits and additional perspectives that are gained from periodically completing individual and couple assessment tools. Although we've been married about forty years, we continue to adjust to each other's idiosyncrasies, moods, preferences and changes that time exacts. Sometimes we easily breeze through a particular season of life and other seasons are more difficult to navigate. It has been especially helpful during the difficult times in our marriage to reach out for assistance.

Reaching out has taken on many forms over the years. It has resulted in one or both of us scheduling sessions with a Christian counselor or therapist, seeking assistance from and being completely transparent with a skilled seasoned couple, or together scheduling time away to talk through and review the results of the assessment tools that we have previously taken. All of these avenues provide an outside or expanded perspective which proves to be helpful—often resulting in rich learning experiences and receiving fresh perspective for the way forward.

Approximately five years ago, we completed a couple's assessment tool that measured the vitality of our relationship. We were astonished to learn what we collectively shared with "fun" and "play."

> The old adage that "couples who play together stay together" is noteworthy.

At times we work and expend ourselves until significant tiredness sets in, which caused one or both of us to become irritable with each other. The assessment results indicated that as a couple, both of us tend to put aside "play" and "fun" until we accomplished the projects, the day's work or finishing our to-do lists. In short, we deferred play and fun until the work was done.

Because we both are responsibility-prone and hold leadership roles, we are inclined to schedule and make room for fun only after we had worked sufficiently hard and felt we earned it. As we shared this finding with other couples in leadership roles, we found that this tendency is quite common. It also became apparent that the work ethic ,and its cultural value in our region, is a contributing factor. Our region's culture esteems the importance of work and achievement, over engaging in play.

Changes that we've made aren't radical, but we have intentionally learned how to "play" hard, as well as work hard. We thoroughly enjoy our work and play. Fun, humor and light-heartedness has also become more infused into our lives. We think of ways to make each other laugh. We plan and make room for fun while working together. Sometimes we even agree to play first and then focus on work.

The old adage that "couples who play together stay together" is noteworthy. Having fun and playing together in a relaxed manner, develops friendship. Couples who consider each other close or best friends, genuinely enjoy spending time together. They typically share a close emotional connection that strengthens the spiritual, intellectual and sexual aspects of their marriage.

REFLECTION
Have you learned to play hard?

Mutual liking, as well as enjoyment of time spent together as friends, is critical to living out marital commitment. Proverbs 17:17 (NLT) reminds us that "A friend is always loyal."

Now our normal routine is to schedule a fun activity on a weekly basis, and to make a point of making each other laugh. Our commitment is not only to have an enduring marriage, but to have one that is filled with enjoyment and times of fun together as best friends.

CHAPTER 7

Relationship Rescue

Wallace and Linda Mitchell

DAY 1

Building Relationship

"Now as they went on their way, Jesus entered a village. And a woman named Martha welcomed him into her house. And she had a sister called Mary, who sat at the Lord's feet and listened to his teaching. But Martha was distracted with much serving. And she went up to him and said, 'Lord, do you not care that my sister has left me to serve alone? Tell her then to help me.' But the Lord answered her, 'Martha, Martha, you are anxious and troubled about many things, but one thing is necessary. Mary has chosen the good portion, which will not be taken away from her'" (Luke 10:38–42 ESV).

> Enjoy the ride and build the relationship.

When my wife is communicating a goal, she tends to be very sensitive to the relational aspect of achieving that goal. A case in point happened one evening while Linda and I were in a very difficult season of our lives. Tensions were running high. Linda mentioned that we needed to purchase a new coat for our son, and asked if I wanted to tag along. I was happy that she wanted to make any kind of connection, so I agreed.

We walked into the store. To the left was the shoe department. She walked into this department and soon we were looking at shoes. Before long, we walked into the next area, which was the shirt department, and we started looking at shirts. Just past that department was the section displaying men's and boy's pants, and we spent time there.

I was starting to get fidgety. I thought to myself, *Maybe I misunderstood why we are here. I thought we were looking for a coat.* I really didn't understand why we were in the pants section. I had to ask, "Were we coming to the store to buy our son a coat?"

Linda said, "Yes."

I just couldn't help myself. I blurted out, "Then what are we doing in the pants department?" Immediately I wanted to pull those words back and stuff them into my mouth.

She gave me a look of disgust and said, "Okay then, we are not doing anything in the store; we are going home!"

We left the store. It was a quiet ride home. Silence was the safest bet at that time.

Some time had passed and again she invited me along to purchase something for one of our children. We walked into a store that had nothing to do with what we had come for, but this time I knew better than to say anything.

During the course of the evening, Linda tried on a pair of shoes and said to me, "These are pretty. I really like these. What do you think?"

Here is what I thought: *I know she has a pair just like those at home. I have seen shoes that look just like them. But I know that's not what I should say or this trip will end, and we'll be home in a heartbeat without getting what we came for.*

So, instead I just answered the question, "I think they are pretty."

She said, "Yes, they are pretty, but I believe I have a pair like them at home," and she put them back on the shelf.

Now how about that, I thought. While I was still puzzled, she was holding up a dress and asking, "What do you think?"

I said, "It's pretty."

She said, "Yes, it *is* pretty." Then she hung it back on the rack and walked off.

Wow, I thought, *I can do this!*

We went through the whole evening like that with Linda showing me something and my commenting that it was *great* or *pretty* or interesting!

I was so focused on the goal of getting what we came for; I was missing the very thing I needed to do in these shopping trips—build a relationship with my wife and have fun in the process. Perhaps I am really thickheaded, but I discovered as a man that it was not a time to simply patronize my wife on shopping trips until we actually purchased what we came for. But, it was the process of walking, looking, dialoguing, listening and looking

REFLECTION

How can you "enjoy the ride" and build the relationship?

again. For so many years I missed this wonderful relationship building opportunity.

It's hard to believe, but these days I initiate going to the mall and walking around. I just turn a "relational" switch "on" when I walk into a mall. If Linda looks at a ring that's worth ten thousand dollars, I take a deep breath and just answer the question, "That's pretty."

I'm secretly hoping she doesn't ask that second question, "May I buy it?"

Facts Do Not Penetrate Emotions

DAY 2

"And there arose a sharp disagreement, so that they separated from each other. Barnabas took Mark with him and sailed away to Cyprus" (Acts 15:39 ESV).

There should be a Bible chapter and verse for this principle, a *Thus saith the Lord*, but I haven't found it yet! The principle is: *Facts do not penetrate emotion*. We each need to grow in our understanding of this concept.

Often men try to fix the situation with "facts" because that is what he knows to do. The facts go from his mouth, hit her emotions and ricochet off into the ozone.

> Laugh with and cry with one another in order to help each other.

In these cases, when a woman is in an emotional state and a man presents the facts, they rarely are able to reach the woman's mind in order for her to sort out and deal with them. The words ricochet off the emotions and rarely penetrate. For example, a husband is mowing the lawn and his wife pulls her car into the driveway. She exits the car and is really upset and shaken. She exclaims, "Someone hit me when I stopped at the traffic light on the way home."

"Are you OK?" he asks. After assured that she is not hurt, the husband quickly glances at the car and sees that not much damage has been done. There is a broken taillight and a small dent in the fender. In an effort to reassure his wife he says, "Well, we don't have to worry about it; we have insurance." His wife is not comforted at all. In fact, she seems a little angrier and repeats the details of the accident again.

The husband, thinking that maybe she didn't hear him the first time, says, "There's no need to be angry; we have insurance."

Now, not only is she angry about the accident; she's upset with her husband. Quickly she turns toward him and states abruptly, "You care more about the car than me!" and stalks off.

The husband, fed up with her responses, says something like, "You're so irrational, no one can talk to you!"

Does this sound familiar to anyone? How can we as married couples grow in this area of misunderstandings? For one thing, we can recognize that *facts do not penetrate emotions*. If the husband could step back, he would realize he could do three things to help in this all too familiar situation.

Recognize the emotion. He should call his wife's emotion what it is—anger. "I can see you are angry." In saying that, she hears that he heard her. His wife needs to recognize that since her husband was not in the accident, his response is going to be less emotion filled.

Validate the person. When he validates his wife, he is saying that the feeling is legitimate. "I can see why that made you angry. I would have been angry, too." That says the husband understands.

Be available to the person. "Is there anything I can do?" This communicates that the husband cares. He is making a connection. The wife feels he cares about what she has experienced.

Now the wife will more than likely say, "Well, it will be okay because we have insurance. They will take care of the car."

This whole incident is not about the insurance. Neither is it about the car. It is about her and what she is experiencing and a husband's response to her needs! A husband will remain in trouble if he does not realize what the real issue is—his wife needs to feel loved, protected, and understood. A wife needs to accept that her

REFLECTION
Did you ever experience a time when facts did not penetrate emotions?

husband will move rather quickly to repairing the car after he is assured that she is not injured. In these types of situations, husbands need to stop leading with statements like,

"We have insurance." She knows, "We have insurance!"

This even applies to emotions related to happier circumstances. Suppose your wife's mother sends your wife an heirloom vase that has been in the family for years. You state that it is the ugliest vase you ever saw! Your wife interprets your words as a direct attack on her mother, even though you were just stating it was an ugly vase. A husband's more proper first response would be, "Oh, isn't it nice of your mother to think of you?"

A husband must realize he does not need to state a factual answer to everything that comes up. The first, and most important, connection with his wife must be relational. After that he can discuss the facts.

Clearly, we are not saying that guys are entirely unemotional or insensitive. The same can happen to them in an emotional situation, because even with men "facts do not always penetrate emotion."

Reach Full Potential

DAY 3

"But we were gentle among you, like a nursing mother taking care of her own children. So, being affectionately desirous of you, we were ready to share with you not only the gospel of God but also our own selves, because you had become very dear to us" (1 Thessalonians 2:7–8 ESV).

"Declare these things; exhort and rebuke with all authority. Let no one disregard you" (Titus 2:15 ESV).

As a wife, I desire that my husband reaches his full potential. Consequently, I encourage him in the way God created him. God made him to *lead, protect and provide.* My husband is motivated by those things and does well when he is achieving in those areas.

It helps when a wife communicates to her husband that she needs him to take the leadership in their family. These humble and submissive words will encourage him to step up and embrace the full capacity of the leadership role God intended for him.

> A husband encouraged to kill dragons will learn to be sensitive to his wife.
>
> A wife who encourages "Dragon slaying" will feel more secure and protected.

Inherently, in a man's heart, he desires to move toward protecting his wife. When she lets him know she needs protection, he is energized to step up and fulfill his God-given role.

A husband needs to be in a position where he feels a necessity to provide. If a husband has the sense that he must provide, he will normally accept the challenge.

Most men are wired to do well under pressure. They may complain, but they'll begin to pull the issue apart and look for solutions. If a wife understands this about her husband, she can help him reach his full capacity.

A man is made to kill dragons! Rarely do you see a woman killing a dragon in a fairy tale. Why does the story of the knight killing the dragon and saving the princess touch a man's soul? Because it fits; it's how his Creator made him.

Several years ago, the Marines had a recruiting commercial depicting a guy killing a dragon. They knew that young males would be enamored by the idea that they could be a hero. You give a guy a sword, and he wants to kill a dragon.

Imagine with me that a knight is trying to kill a dragon with a sword in his right hand, but in his left hand, he has a dove he is attempting to protect. That dove symbolizes a woman. It's not in a woman's nature to fight the dragon; she has her husband to protect her. It's not that a woman couldn't kill the dragon—she doesn't need to kill the dragon. The man will kill the dragon because he needs to.

Picture the husband shouting and grunting as he fights the dragon with his right hand while periodically turning and speaking softly to the dove, making sure she is safe and secure in his left hand. If he shouted and screamed at the dove in the same way he yelled at the dragon, the dove would struggle to get away. The knight learns how to fight the dragon and then sheath his sword, all the while gently talking to the dove.

REFLECTION

How does encouragement make you feel more secure and protected?

The hard part for the male is not in killing the dragon; it

is talking kindly to the dove! He is not the best at displaying those sensitive emotions. At the same time, women learn to understand that a man does not suffer emotional damage from slaying the dragon. What he'll need is appreciation for slaying the dragon and positive reinforcement to do it again the next day.

It's a difficult place for a man to be. He is made to kill dragons, but he must also learn to be relational and more sensitive to his wife.

Unspoken Irritations

"For as high as the heavens are above the earth, so great is his steadfast love toward those who fear him; as far as the east is from the west, so far does he remove our transgressions from us" (Psalm 103:11–12 ESV).

It is often observed that current conflict builds on past conflicts. A husband and wife may believe they are having a disagreement about one particular situation, when in fact it is associated with a multitude of past experiences. It's like a computer program that you start with one click of your mouse, but when the program opens, it includes the information that had been previously entered.

> Unspoken irritations accumulate and color future communication.

Sometimes a man doesn't understand all the issues related to the discussion because he tends to think about one issue at a time—the current one—instead of recalling past unresolved conflicts.

We have seen couples in counseling get into an argument with each other, and we have no idea what they are talking about. We can't follow the dialogue because the couple is speaking in one-word codes.

They have learned over the years to argue with key words. They have only to speak one word, and it can bring up a whole history of past hurts. After years of unresolved issues, a couple can become experts at this type of arguing.

During a counseling session, resolution may be in progress until one spouse says something such as, "Well, you remember the time we went to Georgia. . ."

"Georgia!" the other spouse explodes. "How about Disneyland or Washington D.C.?"

Suddenly, both are furious. One spouse continues, "Well, how about Jane?"

The other one sarcastically quips, "Jane? What about Joe, or Ted or Nick?"

No complete sentences or thoughts are included in these arguments, only words that present pictures of past, apparently unresolved grievances. Only one word is needed to revive all the past emotions related to the event. One such situation came up years ago when I was a young pastor. The couple I was counseling was older than I, and they were angrily batting words back and forth. I was trying to help them resolve a difficult situation and help them better understand each other.

After a bit, I heard what I thought seemed to be the root problem. It sounded to me as if the woman had misunderstood her husband in a particular situation. I thought to myself, *"Great, I can explain this to her, and she will be perfectly happy with my explanation and understand where she misunderstood her husband. Then everyone will be pleased with my wisdom."*

After I explained my great insights, the woman glared at me. Her comment absolutely floored me: "Well, that may be true, but he didn't come to little Johnny's christening."

How in the world did she connect the subject they were discussing with little Johnny? I knew Johnny, and he wasn't little anymore. In fact, he was 30 years old! The couple continued to argue while I sat in front of them speechless.

Eventually I realized that in this woman's religious background, having a child christened was a huge event, with extended family attending the celebration. When the husband refused to attend, it was both embarrassing and insulting to her.

REFLECTION

How do unspoken irritations accumulate and color future communication?

Bitterness grew in her heart for thirty years because her husband had refused to attend the christening. Practically every argument they had from then on was built on that deeply hurtful occasion, because it had never been resolved.

Because her husband's refusal to attend his son's christening was so painful to her, she decided that he could never be right about anything. Thirty years later this deeply wounded woman jumped back to this situation that remained unsolved for her.

We encourage you to learn how to resolve issues instead of allowing them to balloon out of proportion and negatively affect your relationship in many areas.

Cherished and Respected

Solomon Admires His Bride's Beauty:

"Behold, you are beautiful, my love, behold, you are beautiful! Your eyes are doves behind your veil. Your hair is like a flock of goats leaping down the slopes of Gilead" (Song of Solomon 4:1 ESV).

The Bride Praises Her Beloved:

"My beloved is radiant and ruddy, distinguished among ten thousand" (Song of Solomon 5:10 ESV).

Men can struggle getting their masculine arms around the word, cherished. Women seem to be capable of better understanding the meaning of the word; however, it's more through something she feels.

I could give you a definition from *Webster's Dictionary*, but that doesn't work because we are talking about feeling cherished. I think the best way to define feeling cherished is the following picture of a dad and his daughter.

DAY 5

Let's say his four-year-old daughter skips into the room with her fancy Easter dress on. "Hi, Daddy!" she says. As he looks at his little girl, his eyes light up with approval and unconditional love.

What this man's heart communicates at this moment shouts to his little girl that she is cherished. He does not need to say a thing. She knows it by the expression on his face and the approval that comes with his outstretched arms.

Husbands, do your eyes light up with unconditional love when your wife walks into a room? Does she know you approve of her as she is without trying to change her?

> God made us to respond to gender specific positive encouragements.

When a husband listens to his wife's feelings and tries to be more understanding, he is essentially giving her the validation she needs. Validation is saying, "You are okay. I care for you. I understand where you are coming from. I can understand why you feel the way you do."

Wives can work on letting husbands know they appreciate their husbands' talents and skills. Why? I (Linda) have discovered that my husband does not necessarily desire to be cherished as I do. What really connects with my husband is when I help him feel like he's my man, and I'm proud of him. A simple statement of "I'm so proud to be your wife," speaks volumes to a man. It motivates him.

Ladies, Ephesians 5:25-33 tells the husband to love his wife four different times. (Read Day 6 to learn more about husbands loving their wives.)

That same section of Scripture does not say anything about the wife loving her husband. However, it does say something specifically to wives. Because wives are made to be sensitive and relational, God does not need to tell the wives four times to love their husbands. God says only one time in this passage that "the wife must respect her husband" (Ephesians 5:33).

When a wife fails to show respect for her husband, including respecting his words or his decisions, she is destroying his confidence. When she is critical and disrespectful, she undermines him at his weakest point. When a wife makes negative comments about her husband's thoughts and opinions, or gossips with her friends about her husband's idiosyncrasies, she is communicating that she does not respect him. Due to the way a man is wired, negative comments like these tear down his sense of personal

REFLECTION
How do you cherish and respect each other?

worth and value, stunting his leadership development in the home.

A wife does well to give her husband opportunities to lead, provide and protect which show him respect. Giving and showing him respect creates a safe environment in which he can carry out his duty to love his wife. When a wife grasps this concept of respect, it will be a huge break-through in her relationship with her husband.

How Should a Husband Love His Wife

"Husbands, love your wives, as Christ loved the church and gave himself up for her" (Ephesians 5:25 ESV).

After ten years of marriage filled with "I don't love you" messages, Linda and I determined living together was too difficult and too painful. After we had been separated for a year and I read Ephesians 5:25-33 about the marriage relationship, something jumped off the page at me. Four times in that section, it tells the husband to love his wife. But it didn't say anything about the wife needing to love the husband.

I thought, "God, why don't you tell the wife to love the husband? Linda says she doesn't love me, and it seems like You are saying, 'so what'! This doesn't make any sense to me!"

> "God, why don't you tell the wife to love the husband?"

I decided to look up what *love* really meant in the original Greek. Everything I read described an *agape love*, an unselfish love, a sacrificial love. I read that a husband should love his wife like Christ loved the church. How did Christ love the church? He died for us while we were still sinners!

I thought, *this sounds unbelievable, but if You say it, Lord, I'm going to do it! I don't really know how this works but I believe You. So if this thing falls apart, it's not going to be my fault.* Little did I know, this would be the best decision about my marriage I would ever make.

I decided to do what Jesus wanted me to do—to love my wife even though she did not love me. If she ever needed anything, I would be there for her in a heartbeat. I really started to pay attention to our relationship. It didn't exactly make sense to me, but I was doing what the Bible told me to do.

Linda later told me that when I treated her so kindly and she was starting to warm up to me, she became afraid and tried to mask her feelings with sarcastic and negative comments. She didn't want to get hurt again.

Another lesson of life: My focus had moved from Linda and her actions to Jesus and attempting to do what He wanted. Therefore, my actions did not fluctuate according to Linda's behavior.

It was a slow process, but by being obedient and continuing to love her unconditionally, healing started to take place in our marriage. We were becoming more and more cordial to one another, and some of the walls between us were coming down after a year and a half of attempting to love her like the Bible

REFLECTION
Why is Christ-like love irresistible to your spouse?

said. It was working and we left our separated lives to be a unit once again.

One day, after Linda and I had gotten back together, I was reading the Scriptures and came across 1 John 4:19: "We love because he first loved us." I flipped back to Ephesians 5:25 where Paul spoke about husbands loving their wives like Christ loved the church and laid down His life for her. Now I could understand why the original language in the Scriptures didn't say anything about the wife loving back, it was understood that it would happen.

When Christ loves us and we begin to grasp that love, we can't help but love Him back. When a husband loves his wife like Christ loves us, she will eventually respond to that kind of love and can't help but love him back! It is a promise God gave. It is like a divine cause and effect, an eternal law. I didn't understand this when God told me through the Scriptures to love Linda when it seemed so hopeless, but I obeyed because God said it.

Because of our human nature, and living in a world that does not promote Christ's values, I understand that not all marriages work out. I thank God for His healing hand on those who have gone through broken relationships. However, Christian marriages should have a much greater success rate. Both the husband and the wife have responsibility, but a husband has an unbelievable impact on a marriage relationship when he displays this kind of self-sacrificing love.

What's on the Radar?

"An excellent wife is the crown of her husband, but she who brings shame is like rottenness in his bones" (Proverbs 12:4 ESV).

When both husband and wife realize being dissimilar does not mean one is defective, they can learn to work together in their uniqueness, complement each other and even enjoy their differences. This knowledge in a marriage relationship is powerful, but how can this connection and interaction happen gracefully?

> A battleship at sea without a radar is inviting destruction.

Consider the analogy of a battleship sailing off to fight a battle: The battleship represents the man with a mission and task; the radar atop the battleship symbolizes the woman who is sensitive and perceptive as the ship moves forward.

The battleship must maintain the focus by heading in the right direction and carrying out the mission. The radar picks up the incoming danger—enemy planes within radar range but as yet unseen to the natural eye. The radar has an extremely important function because the warning enables the battleship to fully arm itself or maneuver out of imminent danger.

That's how Linda and I view a husband-wife relationship. A woman typically picks up on "relational problems" before the guy does, and she tries to communicate those to him.

It is foolish in a "relational sense" when a husband (battleship) says to the wife (radar), "I do not see the problem. There is no need to talk about this anymore. Turn it off." At that, the wife may indeed stop talking and the husband may think, "Ah, finally...peace!" But it would be reckless and eventually dangerous of the ship's captain to tell his radar department that he no longer needs their expertise. Likewise, a false sense of peace can eventually advance destruction in the marriage relationship.

On the other hand, a wife's radar range is expansive and enables her to detect relational issues. When she hears enemy planes coming across the horizon, it is not too late to "man the ship."

Within a marriage relationship, a husband should desire that his wife remains perceptive so she can do her job and pick up incoming signals without interference. As he cares for his wife, she can do what she does best—be sensitive and relational.

Another interesting thing about radar is that it is so sensitive; it picks up everything—including birds or insects in the area. If the

REFLECTION
Describe how a false sense of peace can destroy a marriage relationship.

ship and radar are working in harmony, the wife pulls in the signals, the husband listens and discusses the different sounds with her and acknowledges the various planes, birds and insects.

He may say, "Wow, so you saw that? That is incredible. It was just a bird. It's not going to bother us, but it's great you are sensitive enough to see it." Consequently the wife knows it's okay to be sensitive and funnel the information to her husband because he will acknowledge it, big or small, and help determine the best preventative response.

Acknowledging this difference helps to create a more inclusive relationship. Endeavor to understand each other's makeup in order to complement one another through open and honoring communication. Working through and embracing such positive differences can create a greater level of balance within your marriage.

CHAPTER 8

Best
Is Yet to
Come

Larry and LaVerne Kreider

Big Three: Communication, Sex, Money

Couples face three main issues that can strengthen or break a marriage: communication, sex and money. Again and again through our years of pastoring and training leaders in the nations, we have seen marriages destroyed by issues related to communication, sex and money.

Notice that the big three can become twisted versions of legitimate and wonderful ingredients in successful marriages.

- Communication is essential in dealing with every aspect of marriage. Unhealthy communication can destroy a marriage.

- Sex, within its perimeters of marriage, is a wonderful gift. But the emphasis of sex outside of marriage in today's sex-saturated society makes it a challenge to stay morally pure, bringing great devastation to those who succumb.

- Money is one of the ways God blesses us to provide for our needs and to advance His kingdom here on earth. On the other hand, the love of money turns some away from serving the Lord faithfully. If Jesus is not Lord of our money, He will not be Lord of our life.

None of us are immune to temptations. Satan is out to steal, kill and destroy (John 10:10), and he will target our individual and married lives. Adam and Eve, David and Bathsheba and other Bible greats reveal that even those momentously used of God are susceptible to temptations and failures.

With marriage, kids, and working—sometimes two or three jobs to make ends meet—and all of the other responsibilities and potential stressors that pop up, spouses become more vulnerable to three major temptations waiting to derail us. 1 John 2:16 lists these three temptations as sexual temptation (the cravings of sinful man), the love of money (the lust of the eyes), and pride (the boasting of what he has and does).

Years ago, LaVerne and I set up clear boundaries, which serve as safeguards from sexual temptations. We also made a decision that we

> Learn to talk with each other about personal differences regarding sex, money and communication.

would not keep secrets with friends but share them with each other.

Clear communication is a key to hold it all together. We learned to use "I feel" statements instead of attacking each other. For example, if I feel LaVerne puts me down, rather than telling her, "You put me down," I say, "When you say that to me, it makes me feel as if you do not value me." By expressing myself through an "I feel" message, I am not blaming my spouse, but focusing on how I feel about her words or actions toward me.

God loves to bless our families, our businesses, careers, our church and our community as we serve Him. However, a businessperson with a thriving business, or a pastor with a growing influential church, needs to guard his or her heart to avoid the temptation of becoming puffed up with pride. Pride—the boasting of what a person has and does—is one of the greatest temptations as mentioned in the biblical passage 1 John 2:16. We are often tempted to believe that accomplishments at home, work, church or in the community are the result of our efforts rather than God's blessings.

Nothing is more effective in dealing with pride than a spouse who helps to keep us humble. When I was a young pastor on the way home from our Sunday morning church services, LaVerne would sometimes ask me, "How did that message help me cope with raising the kids and the nitty-gritty of life?" Her questions taught me to make sure I was being vulnerable and practical in my approach. Although it wasn't always easy hearing her questions, I am eternally grateful. This clear, honest communication set a pattern for me: Make my teaching and pastoral messages simple, practical and applicable to everyday living.

Learn to talk with each other in humility about personal differences regarding sex, money and communication. How money is spent often causes conflict in marriages. Clear communication is so important. Sometimes differing opinions between spouses erupt into ongoing conflict. If we cannot communicate without getting defensive, we need to ask someone we both trust to be a mediator.

We urge people especially to seek counseling when facing overwhelming situations. For example, couples who face bankruptcy because of poor choices or from business failures or downturns in the economy deal with enormous pressures. They should receive godly counsel to help them deal with negative reactions of blaming each other, God and others. Learning to see God working all things together for good when facing devastating circumstances, is not easy, but necessary. That is why a godly counselor can help.

Definitely seek counseling when a partner is unfaithful. We believe our God is a God of restoration, but the anger and hurt caused by unfaithfulness requires ongoing godly counsel to find healing and restoration. Each situation is unique and requires time and help in examining the many different facets involved.

If one partner refuses to work on communication, refuses counseling and attempts of resolving conflict, what should be done? Find a trusted

REFLECTION
Would you and your spouse benefit from counseling?

counselor and confidant for yourself. Opening up to a counselor and/or someone who has been through these same kinds of life experiences, can be a great blessing and offer fresh perspective in setting boundaries and creating a plan for redeeming your marriage relationship.

When Life Seems to Fall Apart

DAY 2

After extensive surgery to remove a mass, the surgeon told Kara and Ben that the cancer was aggressive, that it would return, that there was nothing more to do.

At first Kara and Ben sat in shocked silence. Then Kara said, "Do not repeat anything the doctor said. No one can know it's cancer. I don't want people looking at me, knowing I'm dying, talking about it and treating me differently. I just want everything to be normal."

If Kara and Ben had known that the first stage of grief is generally denial, they would have been better equipped to handle the situation. But they did not know and out of loyalty to his wife, Ben could not share the terrible secret they hid. They could not even pray about it because she pretended the condition did not even exist.

Not being able to draw strength from family and friends should have forced Ben to draw strength from God. And, he did, at first. But as time progressed, the pain of secretly noticing the advances of cancer in his wife choked the life out of him. Not being able to confide in anyone resulted in Ben becoming more and more withdrawn.

While surfing the Internet, some photos popped up. Pornography was only a click away, and Ben chose it. The luring photos were so engrossing that for a while Ben forgot about the pain of losing his wife, his feeling of helplessness and his inability to change the circumstances. When the emotional pain became unbearable, Ben succumbed to temptation again and again.

Men often view pornography as innocent, a fix for loneliness or not having a sexual partner that agrees with his desires. Men rationalize and justify their behavior by attempting to call it "normal behavior." However, the act of viewing pornography is highly addictive—some psychologists state it is like a crack cocaine addiction. Over time the addiction does not diminish, but tends to intensify.

Pornography in our country is a $4 billion industry. A nationally conducted survey among churches over the past five years revealed that 68% of men view pornography regularly

> Pornography and lust are a drive to serve oneself rather than one's life mate or others.

(Pure Desire Ministries). The largest number of users is 11-17 year old boys—85%, and nearly 50% of young girls (From the web site: *Fight the New Drug*).

The church often tells men and women caught up in this issue that it is solely a moral issue, but studies are showing that it is also a brain issue. Telling men to study more, pray more and simply to think pure thoughts is like telling a drug addict to stop thinking about and pursuing drugs.

Studies indicate that when we are involved in sexual activity, the brain releases a chemical, which is the glue to human bonding. Powerful neurotransmitters, such as dopamine, are also released in the brains of those who watch pornography, which creates a bond with the images that actually interferes with human bonding and sexuality. Consequently men and women who love Jesus can be in sexual bondage due to viewing pornography.

Viewing pornography opens the door of our soul and spirit to spiritual oppression, confusion, hopelessness, hurt, control and domination in evil ways. Women feel betrayed —cheated on— by husbands who use porn. Women feel as though they cannot compete with the images their husbands are viewing. It brings insecurities and can destroy her esteem.

One thing we know from God, the Creator of sexuality, His love is completely satisfying. One thing we know from the evil one is that lust is insatiable and can never be satisfied. Pornography and lust are a drive to serve oneself rather than one's life mate or others.

Viewing pornography may start through curiosity or through simply looking for an escape. But escapes have a way of becoming an addiction and addictions have a way of pulling us away from God, the One who provides a way of escape (2 Timothy 2:26).

REFLECTION
Are you seeking escape or resolution when life seems to fall apart?

Therefore, prepare your minds for action; be self-controlled; set your hope fully on the grace to be given you when Jesus Christ is revealed. As obedient children, do not conform to the evil desires you had when you lived in ignorance. But just as he who called you is holy, so be holy in all you do (1 Peter 1:13-15).

There is never an excuse to be unfaithful to a spouse. Sin is always a choice. But both husbands and wives must realize that failing to communicate honestly with each other, as well as, others and not being transparent has far reaching effects. Make a commitment to the Lord and to your spouse to walk in transparency and be open to those who can pray with you and offer hope, accountability and change. The Scriptures teach us to: "Rejoice with those who rejoice; mourn with those who mourn" (Romans 12:15). This can only happen when we are honest and open. Honesty about our failures to God, to our spouse and to appropriate others is a first step toward change. It brings what is presently in the dark into the light so that Holy Spirit can begin a work from the inside of us to our outward actions.

Please note references of help for this area in Appendix A.

Understanding Seven Stages of Grief

One of the greatest stressors on marriages today is experiencing the grief that comes from suffering loss. When we have a loss in our lives, we often experience deep disappointments that can come from having unmet expectations. Loss can come in many forms—the loss of a job because of a merger or failed business or ministry;

death of a parent, close friend or infant; couples not being able to get pregnant; facing unexpected news from your teen or adult children, and the list goes on and on.

Understanding the seven stages of grief[1] most people experience during times of loss, can help us deal more effectively with the problems associated with loss. It is important to understand that these stages do not necessarily follow in order for each person. Spouses often deal with each stage differently but having a basic understanding of these seven stages of grief can help us better understand each other's pain and find resolution.

> Spouses often deal with each stage differently

1. **The first stage of grief is shock and denial.** Most people react to learning of loss with numbed disbelief. We often deny the reality of the loss at some level, in order to avoid the pain. Shock provides emotional protection from being overwhelmed all at once. This can sometimes last for weeks.

2. **The second stage of grief is pain and guilt.** As the shock wears off, it is replaced with the suffering of unbelievable pain. Although excruciating and almost unbearable, it is important that we experience the pain fully, and not try to hide it, avoid it or escape from it. Often people turn to alcohol or drugs to ease the pain. We may have guilty feelings or remorse over things we did or didn't do during this stage. Life can often feel chaotic and scary.

3. **The third stage of grief is anger and bargaining.** Our feelings of frustration give way to anger, and we may lash out and lay unwarranted blame for the death or loss on someone else. We need God's grace to control this, as permanent damage to our relationships may result if this goes uncontrolled. This is a time when bottled up emotions are sometimes released. We may question, "Why me?" We may also try to bargain in vain with God for a way out of our despair. (For example, promising God,"I will never fight with him (spouse) again if you just bring him back").

4. **The fourth stage of grief is depression, reflection and loneliness.** Just when our friends may think we should be getting on with our life, a long period of sad reflection can overtake us. This is a normal stage of grief, so do not be "talked out of it" by well-meaning outsiders. Encouragement from others is often not helpful to us during this stage of grieving. During this time, we finally realize the true magnitude of our loss, and it can make us feel depressed. We may isolate ourselves on purpose, reflecting on things we did with our lost one and focus on memories of the past. We may sense feelings of emptiness or despair.

5. **The fifth stage of grief is the upward turn.** As we start to adjust to life without the person or dream we lost, our life becomes a little calmer and more organized. Our physical symptoms lessen, and our "depression" begins to lift slightly.

6. **The sixth stage of grief is reconstruction and working through.** As we become more functional, our mind starts working again, and we will find ourselves seeking realistic solutions to problems posed by experiencing our loss. We will start to work on practical and financial problems and begin to reconstruct ourselves without the person or dream that we lost.

7. **The seventh and final stage of grief is acceptance and hope.** During this last of the seven stages of grief, we learn to accept and deal with the reality of our situation. Acceptance does not necessarily mean instant happiness. Given the pain and turmoil we have experienced, we may never return to the carefree, untroubled life that existed before this tragedy. But we can be assured that we will find a way forward. With God all things are possible. We will begin to start looking forward to and actually plan things for the future. Eventually, we will be able to think about our lost loved one or unfulfilled vision without pain and sadness. We will once again anticipate good times to come, and again find joy in our lives.

REFLECTION

Are you and your spouse in one of the seven stages of grief?

Romans 8:28 is still true, regardless of what we have been through: "And we know that all things work together for good to those who love God, to those who are the called according to His purpose."

Keeping Jesus in the Center

DAY 4

The raw loss of losing a child will shake the foundation of the strongest marriages. Some statistics show that 80 percent of marriages dissolve after the death of a child. In most situations, I think it is not the pain from the loss of a child that causes divorce, but the hurt from misunderstandings that erupt between spouses dealing with prolonged stress.

When the Carnahans six-year-old child was diagnosed with cancer, the parents drew on the prayer support of many friends. They were confident that God would heal their child and treatment would not be necessary. But the mass grew. Surgery was required. Long-term radiation treatments and chemotherapy reduced their bubbly child to a mere shadow of her former self.

The toil of watching her listless child, of holding her from the retching produced by chemo, of the hair loss, sent shivers of despair through Jessi. One evening she said to her husband, "I want to trust God, but I have this pit of fear in my stomach that I can't get rid of. What if she dies?"

"Don't worry about it. Just believe," her husband encouraged. "We prayed. Others are praying. God will heal her."

Jessi sensed God's strength and love most of the time. But some evenings, exhausted from the strain of caring for a sick child plus her other children, Jessi collapsed in tears. Ben wanted to encourage his wife, so he quoted Bible verses. At first, Jessi admired her husband's strong faith.

She sought stability in God. But again and again, she felt exhausted physically, mentally and spiritually. Frequently her husband chided: "Be strong. Don't worry. Trust God."

When their daughter's MRI scan showed the cancer was expanding, Jessi sobbed, repeating the words, "Why? Why?"

> When we feel weak ourselves and our spouse isn't helping us feel stronger, we often say hurtful things.

"It's your fault," her husband said. "You're doubting; you're not believing." Jessi resented her husband's inference that she was not trusting God. Jessi no longer considered her husband a safe place for confiding her feelings. She withdrew emotionally from him and the problems within their relationship escalated.

After the death of their daughter, the Carnahan's marriage was in shambles. Fortunately, they made a nonegotiable decision that their marriage would not end in divorce.

John had not meant to hurt his wife with his accusation that she did not believe. As previously mentioned, husbands often feel the need to fix things. John wanted to "fix" his family's situation. He was looking for explanations about why God allowed an innocent child to suffer. In frustration John blamed his wife's lack of faith for the circumstance because he hoped everything would be "fixed" if she only believed.

We are to be each other's helpmate, but when we feel weak ourselves and our spouse isn't helping us feel stronger, we often say hurtful things. We are impatient. We blame each other. This behavior generally intensifies when we experience long, difficult times. Instead of blaming Jessi, John should have remembered that Romans 14:1 tells us to "Accept him whose faith is weak, without passing judgment on disputable matters."

Jessi needed to forgive and not harbor bitterness in her heart towards her husband despite his insensitivity. Whenever we feel hurt from a spouse's words, we need God's grace to enable us not to harbor resentment. If we fall short and refuse to forgive, a root of bitterness can spring up in our marriages that can not only destroy us, but our marriages and entire families (Hebrews 12:15).

Marriage is to reflect how Christ responds to his church. A godly marriage mirrors this relationship for others to see. Jesus constantly forgives and blesses, regardless of how others affected him personally. In Luke 23:34, we read, "Father, forgive them, they do not know what they are doing." Jesus calls us to do the same.

We all go through seasons of really difficult times in life that can either make us or break us. If there is any one thing that we want to pass on to other couples, it is simply this: No matter what happens, keep Jesus in the center of

REFLECTION

How has prolonged stress affected your marriage?

your marriage. "Be devoted to one another in brotherly love. Honor one another above yourselves" (Romans 12: 8, 10).

DAY 5

Divorce, Remarriage, Blended Families

"When we married, we knew we'd face some problems with our blended families, but I never envisioned this," Margie said of the dissention within the family.

Al's children lived with their mother and visited him on weekends. "The children's visits put a strain on our relationship, but I forced myself to overlook a lot because it was only during the weekend," Margie said. When the relationship between Margie and her stepchildren did not improve, her stuffed emotions ballooned to the breaking point.

Al's teenage son complained about the food, the activities, Margie's children, everything she did or did not do. . . . Al did not intervene. His silence, from Margie's perspective, proved he did not love her.

"If Al loved me he would care more about my feelings than his son's. He would not allow his son to talk disrespectfully to me," she said.

Al and Margie's problems are not unique to blended families. All families have good times and bad. Children face any number of disappointments as they grow, but having a new mom or dad can be the most challenging.

Child-rearing is difficult enough without having the multiple problems caused by separation, divorce and adapting to a new family and often to a new environment.

In Steve and Mary Prokopchak's book, *Called Together*, a pre- and post-marital workbook, they write they had discovered from personal interviews with divorced couples and families that the most challenging aspect of remarriage was blending children.

"Children need time to heal from a divorce. Their own feelings of hurt, rejection, separation anxiety, fear and anger must be talked about. It will take time to bond with stepchildren. Older children can be very resistant to this process. They feel the loss of a parent more than they feel the excitement of having a new parent. Don't expect immediate acceptance. Be prepared to be rejected—do not retaliate with rejection on your part and never try to compete with the ex-spouse's relationship with his or her child."

> Children need a loving relationship with parents who aren't entangled in conflict.

The baggage caused by divorce and remarriage requires parents to attain skills in dealing with their children's emotional and spiritual state, as well as their own. Because children are wounded by their parent's divorce and the changes thrust on them, the parent in charge often feels guilty for their role in the situation. As observed in Margie and Al's blended family, guilt often results in a parent becoming more lenient or passive in correcting wrong behaviors in children.

Steve Prokopchak said, "Counseling and helpful input into this situation is imperative or a parent will lose this child in more ways than through a divorce settlement." Steve recalls that a 16-year-old teen offered insight into how many children feel when adapting to blended families. He said, 'This is my dad's choice—not mine. I am an afterthought to what he wants. I want it known that I am not choosing a remarriage, but I have no choice. It's a choice made for me, not with me.'"

To help children adjust to their new reality, you, as parents, need to realize that your child is not a lifelong victim because their parents did not stay married. The past is past. Allow God to begin a new work—a good work—in your lives. "Being confident of this, that he who began a good work in you will carry it on to completion until the day of Christ Jesus" (Philippians 1:6).

Children need a loving relationship with parents who aren't entangled in conflict. Intense conflict between the (birth) parents of divorced families can be one of the most damaging experiences for children. It is imperative for parents to foster cooperation with the co-parent and work to stop conflict.

A newly married mother with a stepson recently said that she found it was important to establish a good relationship with the mother of her stepson. This attitude also encouraged a healthier relationship with her stepson and in her husband's relationship with the child's mother. Attitudes can sow seeds of peace or disruption with far-reaching effects into the lives of extended family members. Strive to do your part in building healthy relationships with all those involved.

Although the enemy may have had plans for evil for you and your family, recognize that God has plans to prosper you. . .to give you a future and a hope (Jeremiah 29:11).

REFLECTION

Is God able to redeem bad situations?

Kids Affect Marriage

DAY 6

Children are a great blessing to any family, but raising children often stresses our marriage relationships, especially during difficult seasons of life. I believe our children have the potential to give us the greatest joy and the greatest pain.

We are blessed with four amazing kids. The first two, Katrina and Charita, were born three years apart. We assumed that was to be it—two beautiful girls. Seven years later, our son Josh was born. Leticia was born three years after Josh. We always felt as though we have two families, seven years apart, with two first-borns.

Raising children was not always easy on our relationship. When Larry returned home after working all day, I often felt as if he was a friend to our children while I, who had been with them all day, was the disciplinarian. This, at times, caused tension between us. One day we sat down together and openly shared our feelings about our differing styles of parenting. We then came to an agreement and into unity concerning a change in how we were going to train our children. The key was to communicate and trust God continually for wisdom (James 1:5).

We had been advised that the most important thing a dad could do for his kids is to love their mom. So I made a conscious decision to do this. Years later, we are pleased to report that our children never doubted that their parents loved and cherished each other.

> Raising children was not always easy on our relationship.

Ephesians 6:4 tells us: "And you, fathers, do not provoke your children to wrath, but bring them up in the training and admonition of the Lord." We made continual efforts to give lots of encouragement and proper loving discipline to our children, and then, asked God for grace to not "provoke them to wrath." Provoking a child to wrath (harboring a spirit of anger towards parents) happens when we speak out of anger and frustration rather than with words filled with grace and hope. Each of our children gave their lives to Christ at a young age, but during their teenage years some of them certainly stretched our parenting abilities. We can look back and laugh about many of the incidents now, but parenting is certainly not for the faint of heart.

A friend from New Zealand said, "If you are going to raise kids who are world-changers, they might try to change your world first!"

Choose to enjoy and fully embrace each season of child-rearing for soon it will pass. When our first two babies required nightly feedings, LaVerne often felt guilty for not spending as much time alone with God as she did before having children. A wise woman of God who was a traveling minister told LaVerne one day, "The most godly thing you can do in this season of your life is be a mother." That advice set her free. LaVerne learned to practice the presence of God in the midst of her daily mothering responsibilities.

REFLECTION
Do your children know that you and your spouse love each other?

Today, looking back, we are so grateful to the Lord for his grace. We find our children are grown and are amazing in spite of their parents' shortcomings.

LaVerne and I are so delighted that we took time to build a strong marriage while raising them. Today we are enjoying the good fruit of a blessed marriage.

More in Love than Ever

I remember getting off the plane in Japan on my way to the Philippines. I received a call from LaVerne reporting that our basement was flooded. I wanted so much to be home taking care of this for LaVerne, but I was thousands of miles away. God provided a few friends who assisted LaVerne and temporarily repaired the problem until I could get home a few days later. Incidents like these have taught us that our first trust must be in the Lord, not in our spouse.

LaVerne and I would love to be together 24/7, but we refuse to compare our situation to other couples who are together all of the time. In 2 Corinthians 10:12, the Bible tells us not to compare ourselves with others. We believe it is unhealthy to compare our marriage with someone else's. Instead, we thank God for His grace on our lives to often be apart for short periods of time. We know we are obeying God's call for us. Every couple needs to do the same. Our God gives grace for each situation.

What happens when your spouse, who is in charge at work throughout the day, refuses to make needed decisions when he or she returns home? Can you talk about this or a similar scenario openly and honestly? Are you clear and in agreement about your roles in your home?

For example, who handles the finances and bookkeeping and budgeting in your home? In our family this is my job, not because I am better at it, but because LaVerne enjoys bookkeeping even less than I do. Usually there is not a right or wrong to who does what, but it does need to be clarified.

Our God is calling us as husbands and wives to walk in love toward our spouse. "Therefore be imitators of God as dear children. And walk in love, as Christ also has loved us and given Himself for us" (Ephesians 5:1,2). As husbands we walk in love towards our wives by being godly men, being understanding, praying with them and giving encouragement to them. Wives are called to do the same for husbands. Both husbands and wives need to feel safe with one other, confident that a spouse will not verbally attack or put them down. Be vulnerable and ask your spouse if he or she feels emotionally safe around you.

As a husband, the Lord has shown me the importance of cherishing LaVerne

> We believe it is unhealthy to compare our marriage with someone else's.

and valuing her emotions. 1 Thessalonians 5:23 says; "Now may the God of peace Himself sanctify you completely; and may your whole spirit, soul, and body be preserved blameless at the coming of our Lord Jesus Christ." Our soul refers to our mind, will and emotions. I have found that our wives need to be cherished and valued in their emotions. How they feel is reality to them. Cherishing through encouragement is the vitamin to the soul, bringing blessing and value to the emotions of the one you love.

LaVerne and I have found that consistent prayer times together goes a long way in keeping us connected to the Lord and to each other. Jesus said, "For where two or three gather in my name, there am I with them" (Matthew 18:20). When we pray together, God shows up! Make praying together a priority in your relationship.

This year we will experience 45 years of marriage. We often disclose to people that we had 44 good years and one really tough year. Our God has been amazingly faithful to us. We really are more in love today than at any time during the past 45 years. I heard it said, "'Old love' is just as real as 'young love.'" How true.

While ministering in the state of Texas this past year, I shared with a doctor that I briefly met, "LaVerne and I are more in love today than at any time in our lives." He wrote me a week later to thank me for saying this, because it gave him hope that when he and his wife are our age, they will walk in the same experience.

REFLECTION
How are you and your spouse strengthening your relationship?

We pray God's grace in abundance for you as you keep Him first in your marriage relationship. Our desire is that what God has taught us during our years of marriage will spur you to experience an amazing marriage relationship that will honor the Lord and bring great blessing to many other couples. We speak and declare over you, the best is yet to come!

Epilogue

We are eight authors—with decades of combined marriage experience—who still don't have all the answers pertaining to marriage. What we do know is this: the One who created marriage has the answers for each and every situation.

We also know that each of us loves being married, but our marriages have not been problem free. Through good and bad times, we have come to rely on a healthy dependence upon God and a healthy interdependence with our spouses.

We consented to co-author the book because we believe the insights and counsel that we have had imparted to us may help you also. In the spirit of love, care and hope, we dedicate this book to you, the reader.

As your relationship grows, may your marriage inspire others to be whole and healthy. Commit to allow nothing to come between you and your spouse, to openly and honestly communicate, to pray together frequently, to serve one another and—most of all—to serve the One who gave you the gift of your spouse.

All our love and hope,

Larry and LaVerne Kreider, Steve and Mary Prokopchak, Duane and Reyna Britton, and Wallace and Linda Mitchell

Appendix A

Sexual Addiction Resourse List

Books

The Secret in the Pew: *Pornography in the Lives of Christian Men*, by David A. Blythe
The author draws from his own story from his battle over sexual sin to provide a practical guide built upon God's Word to help others learn how to gain victory.

Facing the Shadow, by Patrick Carnes, Ph.D.
This workbook takes techniques used by thousands of people recovering from sex addiction and shows, in a step-by-step manner, how to break free of this disease and live a healthier, more fulfilling life. Each of this hope-filled work's chapters sets the stage for the recovery tasks at hand, before providing practical, easy-to-follow exercises specifically designed to help understand and address them. Topics covered include: why denial is so powerful and what can be done to counter it; how to face the consequences of behavior using recovery principles; how to respond to change and crisis; how to manage life without dysfunctional behavior; and how spirituality and recovery are interwoven. This is not a Christian model of recovery but can be very effective if used side by side with Scriptural principles.

To Kill A Lion, by Bruce Lengeman
Written by a professional counselor to counselors and strugglers alike, this book provides insight into the root causes of this sin in a person's life and provides solid Biblical insights to help them achieve freedom.

The Pornography Trap: *Setting Pastors and Laypersons Free from Sexual Addiction*, by Ralph H. Earle, Jr. and Mark R. Laaser

Written to address the issue of sexual sin among pastors and lay-persons serving in the church. Provides insight related to when leaders struggle and provides a guide to developing a Biblical view of healthy sexuality.

Healing the Wounds of Sexual Addiction, by Dr. Mark R. Laaser
Traces the roots of the problem of sexual addiction, discusses the impact yet provides a biblical approach to self-control and sexual integrity. This book is essential in helping one uncover the root causes of their acting out in sexual brokenness.

Shattered Vows: Hope and Healing for Women Who Have Been Sexually Betrayed, by Debra Laaser
Written to the wives whose husbands have succumbed to sexual sin through pornography and sexual acting out. Drawing from her personal story of betrayal as well as her experience of help-ing thousands of other women, Debra provides practical tools to empower those who have been devastated by their husband's sin.

The War Within, by Robert Daniels
Provides a powerful strategy for fighting sexual temptation that is based on the promises and power of God interwoven with the author's own testimony of his struggle with sexual sin.

Media
Somebody's Daughter
Provides testimonies of men effected by pornography and how they were able to find freedom. Three men and one couple share how their sexual addiction ravaged their lives, and they also share the freedom they are able to experience because of Christ.

Conquer Series, by Kingdom Works Studios
This is a 5-week discipleship series on DVD hosted by Dr. Ted Roberts. Through a powerful cinematic experience, the Conquer Series has interwoven testimony and sound teaching to provide a

strong battle plan for purity that will benefit any man struggling with pornography and purity. Visit www.conquerseries.com.

Ministries

Day Seven Ministries

Offers individual counseling and group support for men and women in sexual conflict over sexual abuse, sexual addiction, or homosexuality. Locations: Lancaster, Camp Hill, and Reading, Pennsylvania.

Celebrate Recovery

A biblical and balanced program that helps us overcome our hurts, hang-ups and habits.It is based on the actual words of Jesus rather than psychological theory. 20 years ago, Saddleback Church launched Celebrate Recovery with 43 people. It was designed as a program to help those struggling with hurts, habits and hang-ups by showing them the loving power of Jesus Christ through a recovery process. It has helped more than 17,000 people at Saddleback, attracting over 70% of its members from outside the church. Eighty-five percent of the people who go through the program stay with the church and nearly half serve as church volunteers. Celebrate Recovery is now in over 20,000 churches worldwide! Go to www.celebraterecovery.com to find a group near you.

Websites

Fight the New Drug www.fightthenewdrug.org

Raises awareness on the effects of pornography and provides links to the Fortify program, which is an online recovery program developed by them. This is not a Christian organization but does provide useful information on the damaging effects of pornography use on the brain, relationships, and the connection of pornography with the dark world of human sex trafficking.

Endnotes

Chapter 1, Day 4

1. Chester and Betsy Kylstra, Higher Life Ministries: Restoring the Foundations (North Carolina), www.higherlife.org/RTF/RestoringtheFoundationsMinistry.aspx (accessed Jan. 2016).

Week 1, Day 6

1. Gary Chapman, *5 Love Languages* (Illinois: Moody Publishers, 2010).

Week 1, Day 7

1. Dr. Alan Francis with Cindy Cashman, *Everything Men Know About Women* (Missouri, Andrews McMeel Publishing, 1995).

Week 2, Day 1

1. Gary Thomas, *Sacred Marriage*, (Michigan, Zondervan, 2015).

Week 3, Day 7

1. Laura Berman, PhD, *When it Comes to Sparking a Woman's Sexual Desire, Most Men—and Even Women—May Not Know Where to Start* (Boehringer Ingelheim Press Release Archive, May 12, 2010).
2. Dr. Gary Chapman, *Happily Ever After: Six secrets to a successful marriage* (Illinois, Tyndale Publishing House, 2011).

Week 4, Day 2

1. DISC Personality Profile Test. Send for free copy from info@discprofiles4u.comDiSC Profiles 4u 501 Ardson RoadEast Lansing, MI 48823.

Chapter 4, Day 3

1. Dr. Michael G. Conner, *Understanding the Differences Between Men and Women*, (www.oregoncounseling.org) (accessed January 2016).
2. Braindash, www.braindash.com/quotes/dave-meurer (Accessed January 2016).

Chapter 4, Day 4
1. Dr. Daniel Laby, Dr. David Kirschen & Tony Abbatine, *Visual Profile of Major League Hitters*, www.frozenropes.com/core/newsletter_details.asp?ArticleID=76, (accessed January 2009).

Chapter 4, Day 6
1 **Intuition** is the apparent ability to acquire knowledge without inference or the use of reason. (Oxford English Dictionary). Intuition has been the subject of study in psychology. Psychologist Matthew Lieberman published a paper in 2000, entitled *Intuition: a social cognitive neuroscience approach*, and discussed a possible biological basis for female intuition: The hormone estrogen, present in greater quantities in women than men, directly affects the amount of DA [dopamine] released into the striatum (Becker, 1990; McDermott, Liu, & Dluzen, 1994; Mermelstein & Becker, 1995).

Chapter 5, Day 2
1. NerdWallet (October 2015) www.nerdwallet.com/blog/credit-card-data/average-credit (accessed January 2016).
2. Website Debt.org (accessed January 2016).

Chapter 8, Day 3
1. Free download available from www.stages-of-grief-recover com. Permission granted as long as Web site source mentioned

Chapter 8, Day 5
1. Steve and Mary Prokopchak, *Called Together (Pennsylvania, Destiny Image, 2009).*

**Battle Cry for Your Marriage
Chapter 1 Outline**

Trying to Fix Your Spouse
"Ain't Gonna Work"

1. Never Stop Dating
   a. Most important relationship next to God should be our spouse
   b. Focus on good and necessary things may interfere with marriage relationship
   c. Find identity in God, not spouse
   d. Sow into marriage

2. Seasons of Marriage
   a. Larry and LaVerne's courtship, backgrounds that influenced their behaviors
   b. Stresses that affect marriages during various seasons
   c. Don't waste seasons
   d. God is faithful in every season

3. Words Are Dynamite
   a. Let your conversation be always full of grace to show "I care"
   b. Powerful for good or evil
   c. Timing
   d. Pray, let God change them

4. Maintaining Proper Boundaries
   a. Importance of boundaries
       Ex. Time for family, guidelines relating to opposite sex
   b. Establish more boundaries as needed
   c. Be real, don't cover up, walk in wholeness
   d. Marriage checkups

5. Love, Respect, Power of Encouragement
   a. Power of love and respect
   b. Learn how to encourage one another
   c. Power of encouragement
       Ex; Japan empress
       Ex. 50-cow woman

6. Honoring Spouse's Love Language
   a. Five basic love languages: words of affirmation, acts of service, receiving gifts, quality time and physical touch.
   b. Importance of learning to speak your spouse's love language
   c. True love is giving love with no expectancy of return

7. Trying to Fix Your Spouse
   a. Change spouse to become more like me
   b. Plank of pride
   c. Listen, validate spouse's thoughts and emotions
   d. Value, not tolerate differences

**Battle Cry for Your Marriage
Chapter 2 Outline**

Marriage: What Was God Thinking!

1. **Marriage: Creation of God**
   a. Oneness principle
   b. Pursue wholeness

2. **Freedom of Submission**
   a. Greek *hupotasso*, to arrange under
   b. Which spouse is more important?
      Ex. Bridge pillars or surface
   c. Husbands define mission in marriage

3. **Marriage With a Mission**
   a. Marriage mission statement defines purpose, goals, values
   b. Clear mission keeps couples on track, morally, spiritually, financially

4. **Skill of Listening**
   a. Develop listening skills
   b. Concentrate, eye contact, questions, hear whole story

5. Fight, Argue or Pray, Agree

    a. Agreement more powerful than disagreement

    b. Opposing values have positives and negatives

       Ex. Mary and Steve's spender, saver vs. planner/investor and giver

6. Most Intimate Act of Marriage

    a. Praying together reveals heart

    b. Designate times to pray together

7. Three Most Powerful Sentences

    a. I am sorry. I was wrong. Please forgive me.

    b. Why are we quicker to forgive strangers than spouse

    c. Do you want to be right or enjoy your relationship

**Battle Cry for Your Marriage
Chapter 3 Outline**

Under the Covers

1. In the Beginning
   a. God create us with emotional, physical, intellectual, spiritual needs
   b. Develop bond through spending time together, sharing, listening

2. Wow... Are We Different!
   a. Compare generalized gender differences
   b. Spouses need each other's differences
   c. Allow spouse to be herself or himself

3. Spiritual Intimacy
   a. Value spouse. Support each other in prayer
   b. Sacrifice your own needs to create a safe atmosphere for spouse

4. Going Under the Covers
   a. Most satisfying sexual relationships are life-long monogamous married relationship
   b. Sex drive most powerful experience but can be most damaging
   c. Sexual intimacy intensifies marriage relationships

5. **Sex—Get a Head Start**
   a. Critical thoughts about spouse affect intimacy
   b. Brain is main sex organ

6. **Paradox of Sexual Intimacy**
   a. Spouses often rate sex life differently
   b. Dialog and pray about hindrances to sexual intimacy

7. **Sexual Intimacy Starts in Morning**
   a. Words, deeds affect desire for physical intimacy
   b. Actions throughout day affects emotional responses to spouse

Battle Cry for Your Marriage
Chapter 4 Outline

Differences
that Complement

1. **Famiy Culture**
   a. Each spouse has perspective on "best" way to do things
   b. Two right people have problems solving differences

2. **Personality: Opposites Attract**
   a. DISC behavior styles: Dominate, Influencer, Steadiness, Conscientiousness
   b. Differences often cause conflict

3. **Relational Messages**
   a. Women often project two messages: fact and responsive
   b. Men generally more fact, goal driven
   c. Spousal differences generally not intentional

4. **Made to Complement**
   a. One spouse has instantaneous comprehension of multiple details
   b. Another spouse sees only the main thing, not the detail
   c. Learn to use differences to complement rather than divide

5. Short Accounts
a. Accumulated "You are wrong" messages break marriages
b. Reassuring "I love you messages" result in strong marriage
c. Forgive quickly to protect your relationship

6. Truly Listening
a. Learn to understand spouse's personality differences
b. Articulate feelings clearly so spouse receives clear communication

7. Pencil, Flower Analogy
a. Pressure that destroys a flower may not affect a pencil
   Ex: Men and women
b. Spouses often perceive love differently
   Ex. Wife wanted more time with husband, but he thought she needed more things

**Battle Cry for Your Marriage
Chapter 5 Outline**

For the Love of Money!

1. Disagreement We Struggled Through
   a. Spender and Tight vs. Giver and Investor
   b. Merge conflicting concepts to achieve stronger financial base

2. Debt Is Killing Us
   a. Average consumer debt $16,140 straining marriages
   b. Grow assets for financial stability instead of purchasing liabilities
   c. God desires his people to be debt free in order to answer His call

3. Place to Start: It's All God's
   a. Abiding by biblical principles helps avoid financial disasters
   b. Lord gives power and opportunity to attain wealth

4. Creative Budgeting Ideas
   a. Budget shows income and expenses
   b. Generosity and accountability needed
   c. Proper use of cash and credit cards help maintain budget

5. Be Your Own Banker
a. Learn principles for emergency and savings funds
b. Be resourceful in spending and saving
    Ex. Barter items and services. Shop and sell at garage sales, etc.

6. Schedule Money Dates
a. Develop income-producing businesses, grow own food etc.
b. Determine which spouse is better at earning and controlling expenses
c. Set parameters for spending without spousal consent

7. Plan Annual Evaluation Weekend
a. Rewards of righteousness and dishonesty
b. True wealth: family
c. Personal evaluation retreat

**Battle Cry for Your Marriage
Chapter 6 Outline**

Keeping Your Marriage Vibrant

1. **Roommate or Soul Mate**
   a. Nurture marriage to prevent growing coldness
   b. Allow each other to express opinions without criticism
   c. Enjoy shared activities

2. **Are We Really Different Emotionally?**
   a. Accept, admire, respect spouse
   b. Most marriages fail from lack of emotional intimacy
   c. Spouses need affection, acceptance, appreciation, affirmation

3. **Keeping It Real**
   a. Honesty, not avoidance, needed on delicate topics
   b. Pray together, trust God for resolution

4. **Intellectual Intimacy**
   a. Know and discuss each other's opinions, fears, desires, dreams, etc.
   b. Be yourself without fear of spousal rejection, demeaning

5. **Conquering Challenges Through Devotion**
   a. Successful marriage not dependent on "perfect" one but adjusting to spouse
   b. Despite challenges, persevere in faith

6. **Mutual Plans Strengthen Marriage**
   a. Review year by planning a Get-Away
   b. Pray, plan, see how God provides

7. **Reciprocal Fun**
   a. Learn to have fun, play, laugh together
   b. Spiritual, intellectual and sexual compatibility increased through friendship with each other

**Battle Cry for Your Marriage
Chapter 7 Outline**

Relationship Rescue

1. **Building Relationship**
   a. Develop relationship through shopping, mundane chores

2. **Facts Do Not Penetrate Emotions**
   a. Men often attempt to fix, while women tend to talk out emotions
   b. Recognize, validate, be available to hear expressed emotions

3. **Reach Your Full Potential**
   a. Husbands motivated to lead, protect, provide
   b. Wife who encourages, embraces husband's role, feels more secure

4. **Unspoken Irritations**
   a. Current conflicts build on past conflicts
   b. Unresolved issues result in arguing with code words
   c. Bitterness destroys marriages

5. **Cherished and Respected**
   a. Husbands show your love for wife
   b. Wives express appreciation, respect for husband's skill, provision
   c. Do not gossip, mock spouse with friends

6. How Should a Husband Love His Wife
   a. Love your wife like Christ loves the church
   b. Focus on obedience to Jesus, laying down your life unconditionally
   c. Obey because God says it

7. What's on the Radar
   a. Battleship symbolizes man with a mission; radar woman who is sensitive, perceptive
   b. Each spouse's unique traits needed to balance the other's and complete God's mission

**Battle Cry for Your Marriage
Chapter 8 Outline**

The Best is Yet to Come

1. Big Three: Communication, Sex and Money
   a. Bible characters and Christians today often ensnarled by one of big three
   b. Pride—the boasting of what one has or does—is one of greatest temptations
   c. Seek godly counselor to help with ongoing marital conflict

2. When Life Seems to Fall Apart
   a. Pornography often an escape from feelings of helplessness
   b. Pornography like drug addiction; affects brain patterns; destroys marital relationships
   c. Confess sin to God, spouse, godly counselor; be accountable

3. Understanding Seven Stages of Grief
   a. Loss causes shock, denial, pain, guilt, anger, depression, upward turn, reconstruction, acceptance, hope
   b. God offers a way forward despite loss

4. Keeping Jesus in the Center
   a. About 80 percent of marriages fail after loss of child
   b. Spouses deal differently with prolonged stress.
   c. Keep Jesus as the center; forgive, bless, pray with spouse

5. Divorce, Remarriage, Blended Families

a. Blended families most difficult adjustments in remarriage

b. Develop healthy communication with all involved. Family counseling recommended

c. Realization that the past is past. Allow God to do new work in your lives

6. Kids Affect Your Marriage

a. Raising children not easy on marriages

b. Most important thing is for parents to love each other, gives stability to children

c. Being a parent is the most godly thing for this season of life

7. More in Love than Ever

a. Refuse to compare your marriage with others; God gives grace for each situation

b. Cherish, encourage each other

c. "Old love is as real as young love"

Reflection journaling space

Chapter 1 **Trying to Fix Your Spouse
"Ain't Gonna Work"**

Day 1 *Do you look to the Lord for your primary fulfillment (emotional needs to be met?) or do you have a tendency to look to your spouse for this? Explain.*

How are you presently sowing good seed into your marriage relationship in order to maintain intimacy, connectedness and open communication?

Day 2 *What are some of the seasons you have experienced in your marriage?*

Is anything causing extra stress in the season that you are presently experiencing?

Day 3 *What does it mean to speak words that are filled with grace?*

How can we change our behavior if we find ourselves trying to change our spouse?

Day 4 *What are some boundaries the Lord has given to you to keep your marriage safe?*

When is the last time your marriage had a checkup with a marriage mentor or counselor?

Day 5 *Give some practical ways you can love and/or respect your spouse?*

Why is it important to encourage our spouse regularly?

How do you plan to do this?

Day 6 *What is your spouse's primary love language?*

What is your primary love language?

Day 7 *What are some of the most obvious ways that you and your spouse are different?*

How have you tried to fix your spouse?

Reflection journaling space

Chapter 2 **Marriage: What Was God Thinking!**

Day 1 *How long into married life did it take you to discover that, "Marriage is not about me?"*

Discuss the principle of oneness, such as "Steve is Mary and Mary is Steve" as you insert your own names.

Day 2 *Prior to this teaching, did we have a wrong perspective of the biblical term submission?*

Discuss the thought: "Together they (husband and wife) are equally important; you cannot have one without the other."

Day 3 *Describe your marriage mission statement: purpose, goals and values.*

Day 4 *Are you naturally a "teller" or a "listener?"*

How can we work on skills of listening to one another?

Day 5 *Do you fight and argue or pray and agree?*

Day 6 *What are some creative ideas to help us engage in regular times of prayer?*

What are some of the areas that we would like to pray about?

If prayer is the most intimate thing we can do together, how can we guard and maintain it as sacred within our relationship?

Day 7 *Why is it so difficult for me to say those three sentences to my life mate?*

How does pride get in the way of my ability to admit that sometimes I am wrong?

Reflection journaling space

Chapter 3 **Under the Covers**

Day 1 *In what ways do we meet each other's needs for intimacy?*

How does our marriage serve as a positive example of being a close husband and wife relationship?

Day 2 *How can our differences strengthen our relationship with God?*

How can our unique differences assist us in expanding God's Kingdom?

Day 3 *In what ways can we strengthen our shared spiritual connection?*

What specific measurable goal can we agree upon that will result in us enjoying times of prayer together?

Day 4 *What affirming words would we use to describe our sexual relationship?*

Are we meeting our sexual intimacy goals that we mutually desire?

Day 5 *Are there negative thoughts toward your spouse that need to be changed?*

What admirable, desirable, worthy of praise, or lovely thoughts can you bring to mind about your spouse that can spark romantic feelings?

Day 6 *What are intimacy barriers in your relationship? If asked to describe the most intimate moments you've shared together, what comes to mind?*

What are some nonsexual ways of touch that each of you enjoy?

Day 7 *In what ways can we stoke the fire of intimacy or fuel romance throughout the day?*

How easy or difficult is it for us to communicate our intimate sexual feelings and desires to each other?

Reflection journaling space

Chapter 4 **Differences that Complement**

Day 1 *What are some unique family patterns that each one of you has brought into your relationship?*

How are you creating or how have you created adjustments that fit for the two of you?

Day 2 *What is your spouse's personality?*

What encouragement and challenges has your spouse's personality been for you?

Day 3 *How does understanding the phrase "relational message" help your communication as a couple?*

Discuss a time when missing the "relational message" hindered your communication.

Day 4 *Have you as a couple ever had a "dogwood tree" experience?*

How have you at times allowed your differing views of detail come between you?

What is your unique attribute or complementing piece of the puzzle to your relationship?

Day 5 *For you, what are some "I don't love you" straws? (Or "I don't care" or "I am not interested" straws).*

Can you give examples of "I love you" straws?

Day 6 *What are some "red flags" in your relationship that alert you to listen more intently?*

How can you listen more effectively in order to hear the deep and intimate emotions your spouse is communicating?

Day 7 *What does the analogy of the pencil reveal to you in your relationship?*

What does the analogy of the flower reveal to you in your relationship?

Reflection journaling space

Chapter 5 **For the Love of Money!**

Day 1 *How about you? Have you discovered differing financial values?*

How are those differences exposed?

Day 2 *What are your values on personal debt?*

How are you growing assets versus liabilities?

Day 3 *Who is lord of our finances?*

Are we looking to God for our cooperative financial decisions?

Are we sharing with others in need and practicing generosity?

Day 4 *Have we misused our credit cards?*

How can we change our use to be free of consumer debt and stop paying high interest rates on monthly balances?

Day 5 *What can we do differently to spend less and save more?*

How can you acquire more assets rather than liabilities?

Day 6 *Is one of us better at administrating finances and, therefore, better at watching the budget?*

How is our way of dealing with financial matters either increasing or eroding trust in our marriage?

Day 7 *Are we operating in integrity in all areas of our lives?*

When can we initiate our time of annual evaluation and vision casting?

Reflection journaling space

Chapter 6 **Keeping Marriage Vibrant**

Day 1 *In what ways can we strengthen our emotional connection?*

What words or non-verbal gestures do we often use in expressing our feelings of love toward each other?

Day 2 *In what ways do we demonstrate acceptance of each other's feelings?*

What has hindered us from deepening our level of emotional intimacy?

Day 3 *Are there things that hinder you from engaging in difficult conversations?*

Can you identify them and then share them with one another? What difficult conversation have you avoided?

Day 4 *Do you and your spouse hold completely different ideas about a particular topic?*

Can you discuss those areas without attacking your mate's thought process?

Do you enjoy sharing and listening to each other talk about various topics, including those in which you have little interest or knowledge?

Day 5 *Think about a few of the most meaningful victories or triumphs you've experienced together and discuss them with a spirit of thanksgiving.*

As a couple, what dreams have you dreamed about that have yet to be fulfilled?

Day 6 *What mutual or shared plans are fueled by your heart's desire for your immediate (within the next year) or long-term future?*

Are they written down along with time-frames for them to happen?

Day 7 *Who are the couples who inspire you to have a more vitalized marriage because of the relationships they model?*

What can you do as a couple to increase the amount of fun and enjoyment in your marriage?

Reflection journaling space

Chapter 7 **Relationship Rescue**

Day 1 *Discuss why it is challenging, but important, to answer relational questions?*

Has your perceived goal diminished your ability to be relational?

Day 2 *As a couple, has there been a time when, "Facts did not penetrate emotions"?*

How could you have handled it differently?

Discuss how both men and women identify with the importance of the following:
- *Recognizing the emotion*
- *Validating the person*
- *Being available to the person*

Day 3 *When have you applied the lessons in the analogy of the "dragon and the dove"? If you have not, how can you apply them in the future?*

How can you encourage each other to reach your full potential?

Day 4 *When has an accumulated "list" of events confused the current specific conversation that you were having as a couple?*

How did you resolve it?

Discuss an unresolved or past hurt that stirs a painful emotion within you.

Day 5 *Share how a husband showing his wife that she is "cherished" makes a difference in a marriage?*

When and how do you cherish your wife?

How does a wife showing her husband that he is "respected" make a difference in a marriage?

When and how do you respect your husband?

Day 6 *Love is an action. Discuss actions that show you are communicating love to your spouse.*

Share some reasons why you believe the Scriptures tell a husband to love his wife like Christ loved the church?

Day 7 *As a couple, when has your "battleship and radar" worked well together?*

How did you complement each other?

When has your "battleship and radar" not worked well together? What went wrong?

Reflection journaling space
Chapter 8 **Best is Yet to Come**

Day 1 *Which of the big three—communication, sex or money—is an area where you feel the need to grow in as husband and wife, and why?*

When one partner refuses to work on communication, refuses counseling and all attempts of improvement, what should the spouse do?

Day 2 *Why is it important for a husband and wife to be open and vulnerable with each other and with others who will help walk with them during difficult times?*

How are you accountable to each other in regards to your viewing habits on television and the Internet?

Day 3 *Which of these seven stages of grief have you faced?*

Why is it important for husbands and wives to understand these seven stages of grief?

Day 4 *What are some steps you have taken to keep Jesus in the center of your personal life and in the center of your marriage?*

What happens to us and to our relationships when we fall short of God's grace and refuse to forgive?

Day 5 *For those who are remarried due to a painful divorce or the loss of a spouse, name some things that are important to remember. If you are experiencing or have experienced a blended family, how has it caused you to grow as a parent and as a spouse?*

Day 6 *What is the most important thing a dad can do for his children?*

Should we do anything differently regarding our parenting philosophy?

Day 7 *Explain the differences and similarities between your spouse's and your roles within your home?*

List some practical ways you can walk in love with your spouse until "death do you part."

Larry and LaVerne Kreider

Larry Kreider serves as International Director of DOVE International, a network of churches throughout the world. For more than three decades, DOVE has used the New Testament "house to house" strategy of building the church with small groups.

As founder of DOVE International, Larry initially served for 15 years as senior pastor of DOVE Christian Fellowship in Pennsylvania, which grew from a single cell group to more than 2,300 in 10 years. Today, DOVE believers meet in 350 congregations and in thousands of small groups in five continents of the world.

In 1971, Larry and LaVerne helped establish a youth ministry that targeted unchurched youth in northern Lancaster County, Pennsylvania. DOVE grew out of the ensuing need for a flexible New Testament-style church that could assist these new believers.

Larry and LaVerne teach worldwide and encourage believers to reach out from house to house, city to city and nation to nation, and empower and train others to do the same.

Larry writes for Christian periodicals and has written 38 books that have sold more than 500,000 copies, with many translated into other languages. Larry earned his Masters of Ministry with a concentration on leadership from Southwestern Christian University. The Kreiders have been married 44 years and live in Lititz, Pennsylvania. They enjoy spending time with their four amazing children, two sons-in-law and the five best grandkids in the world.

Read Larry's blog at www.dcfi.org/blog
Like Larry and LaVerne Kreider on Facebook
Follow Larry Kreider on Twitter

Steve and Mary Prokopchak

Steve and Mary Prokopchak, as members of the DOVE International Apostolic Council, help to provide oversight and direction for DOVE churches in the United States, the Caribbean and the South Pacific region. They also serve on the DOVE USA Team.

A Christian family and marriage counselor for many years, Steve earned his Master of Human Services degree from Lincoln University. Mary is a registered nurse and works part-time in her field. Active in politics, Mary's personal cause is to see an end to abortion. Steve and Mary's vision and hearts' cry is to see people made whole in their personal lives, marriages and families. The couple travel regularly, ministering in churches across the nation and internationally, giving people the various leadership and counseling tools they need.

Steve and Mary wrote *Called Together*, a unique workbook specifically designed for couple-to-couple mentoring use and are presently writing *Staying Together*. Steve also authored a series of booklets called *People Helping People,* topics suitable for small groups. He co-authored the book *The Biblical Role of Elders for Today's Church* and is the author of *Counseling Basics* and *In Pursuit of Obedience*. Steve has had articles published in *Charisma Magazine, Ministries Today* and *Cell Group Journal.*

Steve and Mary have been married for 41 years and have three married children. The Prokopchaks enjoy one grandchild and live in Elizabethtown, Pennsylvania. They thoroughly enjoy week-end get-aways in the mountains, a good NASCAR race and praying together.

Read Steve's blog at calledtogether.wordpress.com.

Duane and Reyna Britton

Duane and Reyna have extensive backgrounds in both business and ministry and role-model a cohesive team approach. They provide consulting services through Britton Consulting Group, a business devoted to resourcing leaders and organizations for excellence through times of transition and to advance to the next level.

Duane serves as lead pastor at Hopewell Christian Fellowship in Elverson, Pennsylvania and on the DOVE International Latin America Apostolic Team. During more than forty years of ministry, the Brittons planted an inner-city church, assisted in church planting in Kenya, East Africa and pastored churches in two apostolic networks.

With a Master's Degree in psychology/counseling, Duane's blend of gifts, geared toward equipping leaders and strengthening the body of Christ, include teacher, administrator, church planter, counselor, mediator and international conference/seminar speaker.

Reyna is a registered nurse and has held administrative positions within corporate and non-profit organizations. For several years Reyna served as a senior examiner for the U.S. Dept. of Commerce, assessing businesses pursing world-class recognition through the application of the Baldrige Criteria for Business Excellence.

Both Duane and Reyna travel and speak internationally. They are passionate about assisting developing leaders, equipping leadership couples to experience synergistic marriages and have the joy of parenting many spiritual sons and daughters throughout the world.

The Britton's eight grandchildren are treasured gifts born to their three talented children, one son and two daughters.

Connect with the Britton's at www.brittoncg.com.

Wallace and Linda Mitchell

Wallace and Linda Mitchell have had the privilege of serving in a variety of ministries that have given them a broad view of church service. The most foundational element in the Mitchell's ministry was learned through their marriage difficulties. Married in 1968, the couple later separated for two and one-half years. During that time, Wallace allowed God to teach him through his Word on how to love his wife. Their powerful testimony of God's restoration of their marriage appeared in their book *Not Right, Not Wrong, Just Different*, printed in 2009.

Ministry was not Wallace's first career choice. He worked for the CIA from 1973 to 1989. After accepting Jesus to be Lord of his life, Wallace served as associate Pastor at Reston Bible Church for ten years. The Mitchells were called in 1997 to plant a church in the Ashburn area based on the cell/shepherd group model with an emphasis on empowering and releasing individuals. Wallace, Linda and a small group of pioneering individuals started Broadlands Community Church in January 1998. Since 2004, Broadlands Community church has been a partner church with DOVE International.

The Mitchells' heart for Scripture is steadfast and prevalent in their counseling of other couples. Linda also uses her lay counseling training to disciple women. Wallace and Linda have a passion for people, both as a result of difficulties they have endured and their experience in receiving God's healing touch. The couple has two grown children and six lovely grandchildren.

Other books in this series
When God Seems Silent
Discovering His purposes in times of confusion and darkness. Why does it sometimes feel like God is silent? Is He hiding from us? Is He angry? Larry and LaVerne Kreider help us examine these questions and many of the barriers that can block the voice of God in our lives. They also reveal their own struggle with God's silences and the tremendous breakthroughs that can be discovered. *By Larry and LaVerne Kreider, 208 pages:* $12.99

Straight Talk to Leaders
What we wish we had known when we started. Four Christian leaders disclose key leadership lessons they have learned through forty years of pastoring and establishing worldwide ministries. This illuminating book explores topics such as team building, boundaries, transitions, unity, stress management, learning from criticism, making tough decisions and much more! *By Larry Kreider, Sam Smucker, Barry Wissler and Lester Zimmerman, 204 pages:* $12.99

Other books on marriage
Called Together Pre and postmarital workbook
This unique workbook, specifically designed for couple-to-couple mentoring use, prepares couples for a successful and God-honoring marriage. *Called Together* supplies down-to-earth Biblical wisdom to help couples get off to a positive start. *Called Together* also includes postmarital checkups at three and nine months. Special sections for remarriage, intercultural marriages and remarriages of senior adults. *by Steve and Mary Prokopchak, 250 pages*: **$19.99**

Not Right, Not Wrong, Just Different
It's obvious that whatever they did to restore their marriage worked! Wallace openly shares that story. They lived through a crisis that would destroy most marriages and now are helping other couples build their relationship on a solid foundation while growing daily in love and respect toward each other. *by Wallace Mitchell III, 136 pages.* **$14.99**

Just Not Right, Not Wrong
Different

Wallace Mitchell III

www.h2hp.com
Call 800.848.5892

Made in the USA
San Bernardino, CA
05 April 2016